GOODBYE ANXIETY

A GUIDED JOURNAL FOR OVERCOMING WORRY

TERRI BACOW, PhD

SPRUCE BOOKS
A Sasquatch Books Imprint

Printed in the United States of America

SPRUCE BOOKS with colophon is a registered trademark of Penguin Random House LLC

25 24 23 22 21   9 8 7 6 5 4 3 2 1

Editor: Sharyn Rosart
Production editor: Jill Saginario | Copyeditor: Callie Stoker-Graham
Designer: Alicia Terry
Illustrator: Erin Wallace

ISBN: 978-1-63217-390-4

Sasquatch Books
1904 Third Avenue, Suite 710
Seattle, WA 98101

SasquatchBooks.com

This book is dedicated to Jay, Adam,
Ruby, Lenny, and Marlene

*"The greatest weapon against stress is our ability
to choose one thought over another."*

—WILLIAM JAMES

*"Anyone who has never made a mistake
has never tried anything new."*

—ALBERT EINSTEIN

#GOODBYEANXIETY

CONTENTS

WHY SAY GOODBYE TO ANXIETY?

IF YOU ARE reading this book, you are probably familiar with the emotion that we call anxiety. Maybe just a little bit, or maybe a ton. Quite possibly, your anxiety is quietly a big deal for you, something that pops up and interferes in different aspects of your life. It may not always be a feeling that you are aware of at every moment, but it is likely always there. Anxiety can be stealthy, subtle, and super uncomfortable. However, there is good news—you can make anxiety less uncomfortable if you learn to befriend and manage it! This book will help you do exactly that.

Where does anxiety come from? Anxiety is neurobiological—it originates in our brains *and* bodies. This mind-body connection is why we experience physical symptoms (such as a racing heart, stomach butterflies, and muscle tension) when we feel nervous or scared. Anxiety is also highly genetic—studies show that some people inherit a tendency to experience anxiety more intensely than others. This tendency runs in families and is not anyone's fault—you are born this way!

Everyone on earth feels anxious sometimes because anxiety is actually protective and adaptive. This means that during the evolutionary process, nature decided that feeling anxious might actually keep us safe. Back when people lived in caves, feeling worried about being attacked by a wild animal, for example, led you to appropriately freak out and run away when you saw one. Nowadays, if you are about to cross the street and a bus is hurtling at you, it is probably a good idea to let fear inspire you to swiftly step out of the way. From a safety perspective, having a fearful response to things that are actually really dangerous developed as a healthy adaptation.

If anxiety is so adaptive, why would anyone write a book about saying goodbye to it, or to be more accurate, learning to manage it? The reason is that today, many of us feel overly anxious way too much of the time—and often in situations where the anxiety isn't truly warranted. You don't need or want to be in the grip of fear all the time, or most of the time, or even in response to a particular situation, unless it is truly dangerous. To be

honest, giving a presentation in front of your class or colleagues is not technically a life-or-death situation—and it doesn't have to feel like one!

Anxiety becomes a problem when we experience it on a daily or very regular basis and it starts messing up our lives. If anxiety keeps you from falling asleep, distracts you from school or work, or causes you to cancel or miss out on events, it is interfering with your life. If your feelings of anxiety are distressing and deeply uncomfortable, that is when it is time to look for some help in managing it.

BIOLOGY + STRESS = WHAM!

What causes normal, adaptive anxiety to transform into a problematic feeling? Today, a lot of us experience constant, low-grade stress—and if you never stop feeling stress, then it can become your default setting to be anxious all the time. When stress interacts with a biological predisposition to anxiety, instead of anxiety coming and going, it comes and stays.

Typically, there are three factors that contribute to developing problematic anxiety:

1. Observation: When we are genetically prone to anxiety and then we observe others acting anxiously (such as parents, teachers, or friends who may also have anxiety), we learn from this and may begin to mimic it.

2. Information: The news and social media can be full of scary events; when we are bombarded with frightening news, it's easy to conclude that the world is dangerous and we should be nervous about it.

3. Experience: Almost everyone will experience some kind of anxiety-provoking life event (changing schools or a painful breakup, for example) or even a truly traumatic event (a divorce or serious loss, for example) that can set off an anxious reaction that is hard to let go of.

Any combination of these factors might leave you feeling upset and anxious more often than not—in which case, it's time to get some help.

WHAT IS ANXIETY?

Anxiety is different from fear and worry. Fear is a very present-moment feeling about a current real-world event, while worry is a speculative feeling about something that is potentially in the future. Fear happens when there is a bear in your path right now and you feel scared AF. Worry is when you are fretting about what is going to happen tomorrow, next week, or next year. Worry is a thinking problem: your thoughts tell you that situations (real or imagined) are most certainly going to be negative. Worry is an unavoidable part of being alive, but if it becomes a regular part of your life, it may be a symptom of anxiety. Fortunately, anxiety is something that can be treated with therapy. "Healthy" worry is specific and temporary; anxious worrying is general and persistent.

If you find yourself worrying more days than not, for a period of six months or more, and if you feel that it is difficult to control, you may meet the criteria for Generalized Anxiety Disorder (GAD). This is a very common experience—lots of people have GAD. It is uncomfortable—and can even sometimes make you feel downright miserable—but the good news is that it responds very well to therapy. In this book, I am going to teach you many of the most effective tools used in therapy to vanquish anxiety.

YOU ARE NOT ALONE!

Anxiety is the *number one* condition that is diagnosed by psychologists and psychiatrists. It is incredibly common, and every single person that I work with in my therapy practice struggles with it. Anxiety is especially common in young people—and adolescence is the peak moment for experiencing anxiety. Scientists report that anxiety increases significantly between the ages of twelve and seventeen—and that almost a third of adolescents ages thirteen to eighteen have an anxiety disorder. Anyone who has experienced some anxiety in childhood (and who hasn't?) is likely to find that the stresses of puberty, the teen years, or young adulthood can create a tipping point. In my years as a therapist, I have discovered that adolescents and young adults are not only very frequently anxious, they also seem to experience anxiety *more intensely* than those who are older or younger.

The social pressures that young people face are huge, and that makes feelings of insecurity run very high. There is so much pressure these days to be perfect—to look perfect, act perfect, and present a perfect picture of your life to the world—and if not, to change yourself! This is an impossible standard that is made even more intense by social media. I am not the type to say that we should eliminate social media (just check out my Instagram!), but I do think it has created a culture of perfection that makes the experience of anxiety even more pronounced. Add in everyday stress (and everyone's life is stressful in some way), and we end up with a lot of people who are in need of relief!

It is entirely natural to think you are the *only one* having a tough time. You are not. EVERYONE experiences these same doubts and fears. Many people pretend not to, but they do. So, if you are feeling anxious, know that you are not alone!!

YOU DO NOT HAVE TO SUFFER

Due to the very subtle and ongoing nature of worry thoughts, many of us just sit with our anxiety and suffer through it. It can sometimes feel like it would take too much time or energy to explain what you are thinking and worrying about to a friend or family member. Some of us feel concerned that if we actually shared our worry, people wouldn't get it, or might even judge us. Young people in particular often feel embarrassed and reluctant to share their negative emotions. This is a shame because it is *entirely normal* to have anxiety. Moreover, keeping feelings inside and unacknowledged is not healthy and makes things worse. If we suffer in silence, the anxiety builds and builds. There is a ridiculous stigma associated with anxiety and worry, which is very unfortunate and, I believe, truly unnecessary. We live in a turbulent world (at the time this book is being written, we are still in the midst of a pandemic). Worry is exhausting, overwhelming, misery-inducing, and can reduce your quality of life. It can distract you, rob you of your sleep, make your body feel tense, and reduce your enjoyment of activities. No one should have to just sit with it—and the good news is, you don't have to! This book is going to help you break free of those uncomfortable feelings by learning to cope with them.

BREAKING THE WORRY CYCLE

Worry is a problem with thinking—or overthinking. When you find yourself fixated on a particular issue or event, you may be ruminating, which is one kind of problematic worrying. Ruminative worry takes us out of the present moment, and, instead of focusing on what is actually happening right now, we become preoccupied with potential (and often negative) future scenarios.

"What if I don't do well on my test tomorrow?" "Is it possible to actually, like, fail the SATs?" "What if I don't get into college?" "What if I can't find a job?" "What if my BFF is mad at me and never speaks to me again?" "What if my crush thinks I'm lame?" "What if my parents get sick?"

These concerns are legit and upsetting, but here is the thing: *we don't actually know what is going to happen in the future!* None of us have a crystal ball, yet when we identify some possible future problem, instead of acknowledging that it's just a "maybe," we may instead spend hours speculating about it and feeling deeply worried about it. We might even become convinced that these things will *definitely* happen to us AND that they will be terrible and catastrophic. While it's true that any of these circumstances could be difficult, it is *also* true that very few of them are the absolute end of the world. The truth is that in most cases, if any of your worst concerns came to fruition (which tends to be unlikely), you *actually would be able to handle it.* You could cope.

The real problem here is not the thing(s) you're worried about—it's the intensity and frequency of your worrying. In this book, I'm going to help you break that worry cycle and put things in perspective.

HOW THIS BOOK HELPS TO BREAK THE WORRY CYCLE

STEP 1

Figure out what exactly you are worried about. In order to resolve and manage worry, we first need to *identify what specifically we are worried about.* This may sound simple and obvious, but it is not as straightforward as it seems. Worries can become part of our stream of consciousness, like background noise. Most of the time, those of us with anxiety are walking around every day feeling pretty stressed, aware we are stressed, but not always knowing *why* we are stressed. It is as if our minds are on autopilot

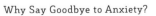

(they are). We are typically not conscious of the specific worry thoughts we are having that are stressing us out because we aren't actively think-ing about our thoughts. They feel automatic to us. These thoughts fade into the background and form the soundtrack of our minds; the volume is low, but still impactful. Yet, the *thoughts* themselves are the very thing triggering your anxiety. *If you have worrying thoughts, you are going to feel worried.*

So the first step is to figure out what, exactly, is worrying you by identifying your anxious thought patterns. That's what we are going to do in Part I and Part II of this book.

STEP 2

Let it out. Scientists have found that the thing that makes therapy so helpful in general is something called catharsis (the release that you feel upon expressing your innermost thoughts and feelings). For most of us, it is *such* a relief to actually say what is on our mind in a safe, private space with an objective, warm, and supportive person present to hear us out! In contrast, keeping these thoughts and feelings to yourself can be such a heavy burden. It requires effort to hold them back, and that puts a strain on the brain and the body.

Research shows that the act of putting your feelings into words can lower the level of arousal in the part of the brain that manages emotions and governs our responses to things that are upsetting. This area, known as the amygdala, lights up when we experience stress. Talking about your problems actually quiets the amygdala, and that enables us to calm down and more logically work through stressful events and situations. Think about the last time you vented to someone you cared about. Didn't you feel so much better after expressing your feelings and talking it out?

Scientists have also found that the act of *writing* down your thoughts and worries—journaling—has a similarly powerful cathartic effect. Specif-ically, putting your thoughts into writing makes a measurable difference

in how you feel. While not a substitute for the personal interaction of therapy, journaling has proven to be an incredibly effective way to release some of your anxiety. Just putting your worries into words and expressing them on paper (or your phone or computer) will start you on the path to feeling less anxious. In fact, researchers have found that setting aside blocks of time to record your worries (known as "worry time") can lead to notable reductions in anxiety.

Studies show that writing about traumatic or stressful events makes people feel calmer, happier, and more at ease. The physical health benefits of expressive writing include things like improved immune system functioning (fewer colds!), reduced blood pressure (a longer life!), and fewer stress-related visits to the doctor. Further, journaling has been found to ease mental distress and increase feelings of well-being even in people with elevated anxiety symptoms. In one research study, it also contributed to improvements in memory and better performance in sports and on tests.

Writing can provide a wonderful outlet to express unspoken thoughts without being judged. You may think, "I can't write," but the truth is that you likely have plenty of experience with writing—texting, emailing, blogging, live chatting, and tweeting are all writing exercises! The difference is that instead of public expression, journaling offers you a private and empowering forum to express your own personal truths.

STEP 3

Take action. While venting in and of itself is an incredibly powerful step, it can be even more effective if you combine it with using clear and concrete strategies to deal with the worry that you are expressing. In this book, in addition to the incredible relief of writing out your worries, you will also learn skills to help you think through your problems, actions you can take to help you feel less anxious, and strategies to keep you from getting overwhelmed by your anxious feelings.

HOW TO USE THIS BOOK

This book includes a series of writing prompts and thought exercises to help you through each stage of dealing with anxiety. Start with Part I, where the prompts will encourage venting, listing, and basically just dumping out your worries! Don't fret about your writing style; just let it all out. The prompts are not just for unloading worries but also to help you with the process of introspection (reflecting on your thoughts and feelings), which is essential to changing how you deal with anxiety.

Part I: What's on Your Mind? encourages you to respond to prompts (questions) that are designed to draw out your concerns and help you figure out what is really bothering you. If a question in this section does not apply to you, feel free to skip it. Since these prompts may not capture every nuance of things you think about (I am not a mind reader or a fortune teller!), there are lots of designated "worry dumps" where you can vent about absolutely *any* topic that is stressing you out. You can dip into this section at any time—and you need not complete the prompts all at once.

Part II: What Can You Do About It? includes a series of prompts designed to teach you coping skills based on the tried-and-tested therapeutic method of examining the evidence for your worry thoughts and determining whether they are truly realistic. This section includes examples of common thinking traps (patterns of thinking) that occur when people worry, and techniques for combating them. You will learn to identify your particular worry traps and answer questions that will help you decide if your worries are truly valid. As a result, you will feel more confident about being able to calm yourself—and with practice, you will likely find that you experience less anxiety overall and can deal more easily with any anxious thoughts that do intrude.

Part III: How Can You Overcome Worry? introduces the most common themes that pop up when we worry and gives you the opportunity to develop and practice your own useful scripts that will replace unhelpful self-talk with more balanced, positive thinking. The more you disrupt your worry patterns with these new, more realistic, self-supportive thoughts (which we will call "coping statements"), the less habitual your anxiety will become. For each aspect of worry that is introduced and described (i.e. dealing with uncertainty, perfectionism, avoidance, and more) you will first have a chance to explore how it comes up for you, and second, learn a coping strategy and review sample coping statements relevant to this theme. If you'd like to, you will also have the option to generate your own personal coping statements that will bring you a sense of calm and relief.

No matter what, these exercises will make you better able to handle the challenges of anxious worry. Most people who use these tools start to feel a lot less anxious pretty quickly. Although I cannot promise you will feel 100 percent better, I am pretty confident that you will experience real relief. If you do not feel sufficiently better or would like to try out in-person (or virtual) therapy (I highly recommend this!), you should feel comfortable seeking out extra help. The Delve Deeper section (page 166) is where you will find more information on the treatment methods from this book, as well as helpful organizations, books, and other sources of information. To delve deeper, please visit my website, DrTerriBacow.com, to find even more resources, including recommended videos, podcasts, social media accounts, and apps to help you learn even more about how to manage anxiety.

Remember, anxiety is incredibly common. You are not alone, and feeling calmer and happier is a worthwhile, achievable goal. You can feel better!

Terri Bacow, PhD

PART I

WHAT'S ON YOUR MIND?

VENT ABOUT YOUR WORRIES
BY RESPONDING TO A VARIETY OF PROMPTS
ASKING YOU ABOUT YOUR ANXIETY.

INSTRUCTIONS: Read the prompts on each page, which are designed to help you figure out what is worrying you. Do not worry if you cannot come up with an answer for a particular prompt—just complete the ones that feel relevant to you. Don't feel concerned about your writing style either; this is just for you and is entirely private, so feel free to let it all out. If you start to feel anxious at any point, stop and take a breathing break.

HOW TO TAKE A BREATHING BREAK

Breathing breaks are awesome! Calming breaths instantly soothe your nervous system. When you are very stressed, you tend to breathe shallowly and quickly, which can make you feel more anxious—but slow, deep breathing, also known as relaxation breathing or diaphragmatic breathing, can quickly break that cycle. Breathing is free and can be done anytime, anywhere, and in pretty much any situation (you won't accidentally forget your breath at home and you can't leave your house without it). When life feels out of control, at least you can control your breath! Here is how you do it:

1. In a standing or seated position, place one hand on your lower abdomen. Inhale slowly and deeply through your mouth or nose.

2. When you have taken in a full breath, pause and gently hold for a couple of seconds.

3. Now exhale slowly through your mouth on a count of four (you can go up to eight if you wish), pursing your lips as if you are about to whistle, to control your exhale. If you'd rather not count, just focus on releasing as much air as you can.

4. Repeat this cycle at least a couple of times.

5. Do this as often as necessary.

Note: Some ways to enhance the calming effect of breathing include saying a soothing word (such as "calm" or "relax") silently to yourself or imagining a relaxing scene (such as a beach or forest or your favorite place) as you breathe. You may also want to try applying gentle, soothing self-touch (such as lightly stroking your arms or putting your hand over your heart). Do this the next time you feel worried and see what happens!

TODAY'S SPECIAL

Has anything been worrying you today? Use the space on this page to describe
whatever it is in detail. What is the worry about? When did you notice it?
How did it make you feel?

TOP 5!

Do you ever feel like your mind is an internet browser? Like, inside your brain, fourteen tabs are open, two are frozen, and you have no idea where the music is coming from? This is typical of worry—often we have multiple concerns happening simultaneously. The key is to figure out *what are the top worries trending in your mind right now.*

List your top five worries here. Put a star next to the ones your mind circles back to regularly.

-
-
-
-
-

#1 WORRY

Out of those five top worries, which one is causing you the most intense concern?

THE STORY OF TONIGHT

Worry, by definition, is concern over things that haven't happened yet. Is there something you are worried will happen today or this week?

....

....

....

....

....

....

....

BACK TO THE FUTURE

Are you feeling concerned about problems or events that may happen next month, next year, or beyond? Write down some things you are worried will happen in the future.

Next month:

....

....

Next year:

....

....

Beyond:

....

....

....

TRIGGER ALERT

Identifying anxiety triggers—things that get your worry going—is helpful when it comes to developing coping strategies. You might be triggered by a particular person (maybe someone you follow on social media whose apparent perfection makes you feel insecure), an upcoming event (a test or even something that you might also find fun, like a party), or a physical sensation (such as a weird pain or feeling in your body that makes you feel freaked out). What are some of your triggers?

I get worried when:

....

....

....

....

....

....

....

READY TO RUN

Are there any places, people, things, situations, or activities that you avoid because they trigger anxiety? List them below.

-

-

-

-

-

CAN'T GET YOU OUT OF MY HEAD

Sometimes you can't stop dwelling on something that is worrying you, as if your worry thoughts are a persistent animated GIF that just keeps on going (and going . . .). Write about one or more worries that have especially preoccupied your mind lately, or that you may be ruminating about.

NO SENSE

Worries can be completely irrational and do not always make sense (no one is judging!). Write down a few of your most ridiculous worries. It is okay if they are utterly absurd. For example, have you ever worried that someone will steal your homework? Are you worried that you will get such bad grades that you will need to drop out and never finish school? Are you concerned that you will get fired from your job for making a careless mistake? Do you ever worry that you will spontaneously combust?

◦

◦

◦

◦

◦

I'VE GOT 99 PROBLEMS AND ANXIETY IS ONE OF THEM

Does worry ever mess up your life? Does it stop you from doing things that you want to do? List a few ways that your anxiety creates problems for you or makes your life less enjoyable.

o

o

o

o

o

BRAIN CELLS

Often we focus our worries on relatively minor issues, like getting a zit or forgetting to pack your toothbrush for a trip, because we believe it is easier to control such things. List some small things that you have spent a lot of time worrying about.

....

....

....

....

....

....

....

....

BIG DEALS

Sometimes our minds get stuck on major problems, like climate change. What are some really big, less solvable issues that occupy your thoughts?

....

....

....

....

....

....

....

BAD DECISIONS

Worrying can make it harder to make decisions. Choices can start to feel scary when we are endlessly questioning the right move. Write about a decision you are having trouble with lately. What are the options? What are the possible worrisome outcomes that you are thinking of?

I don't know what to do about:

....

....

....

....

....

....

I can't decide between:

....

....

....

....

....

....

I am worried that:

....

....

....

....

....

....

WORRY DUMP!

Get it all out. Write or draw anything that is upsetting you. Visualize your anxieties and put them here. Imagine a giant trash can and toss all your anxiety-producing thoughts and worries into it!

THE STORY OF MY LIFE

For many of us, worrying begins when we are little kids or intensifies when we become teenagers. Write about your personal history with worry.

When did it start?

....

....

....

....

....

....

Do you remember seeing, hearing, or learning about something scary or worrisome that stayed with you?

....

....

....

....

....

....

How have people in your life responded when you have expressed worry?

....

....

....

....

....

....

YOU NEED TO CALM DOWN

Anxiety isn't happening only in your brain. The brain sends signals to the body, which means that worry can be a really physical experience. What are some ways you feel your anxiety physically? Check all that apply.

- Racing or pounding heart
- Dizziness
- Nausea
- Restlessness
- Sweatiness
- Stomach butterflies
- Tight jaw
- Tense muscles
- Headache
- Skin breakouts
- Stomachache
- Shortness of breath
- Tingly limbs
- Feeling faint
- Dissociation
- Other _____
- Other _____
- Other _____

WIDE AWAKE

It is very common to have a hard time falling asleep when you're worried. What are some things that you worry about when you are trying to fall asleep or when you wake up in the middle of the night? Do you worry about not getting enough sleep and being tired? Write about what this experience is like for you and any specific sleep concerns that you have.

THE PARENT TRAP

We often worry about the same things our parents or other close family members do. What are some things that your parents, siblings, or caregivers seem stressed about? Do you see any similarities between your worry thoughts and theirs?

COMPARE AND CONTRAST

Is there someone (or multiple people) to whom you often compare yourself?
This comparison process can make you feel stressed and badly about yourself. Fill
in the chart below to explore this habit.

WHO DO I COMPARE MYSELF TO?	WHAT DO I ADMIRE ABOUT THEM?

AS I AM

Sometimes life feels like a competition. We are doing perfectly well, even great—but when we think about other people, we suddenly feel like we are falling short. In the chart below, write notes in any categories where you worry that others are doing better than you. (Remember, they might not be, but list where your worry takes you.)

LOOKS/APPEARANCE:

GRADES/WORK PERFORMANCE:

SKILLS/TALENTS:

POPULARITY:

LOVE LIFE:

MONEY/PRIVILEGE:

FOMO

On social media, it may seem like *everyone* is having a better time than you—but remember, looks can be deceiving! Write about seeing something on Instagram, TikTok, Reddit, Facebook, Twitter, or Snapchat that left you feeling badly about yourself or anxious about being left out. Is this a regular worry for you? How much does it affect your life?

....

....

....

....

....

....

....

....

SEEKING LIKES

It can be soooo stressful to put ourselves out there on social media, yet we still do it. Write about any insecurity you may have about this, such as worrying that people are not liking or commenting on your posts enough or that you do not have good enough content to share, or enough followers.

....

....

....

....

....

....

....

....

BAD REPUTATION

Do you have any concerns about how other people view you? Have you felt stereo-typed in some way? Is your Snapchat score too low or high? Describe your worry in detail—whose opinion are you worried about, how do you think they see you, and how does it make you feel?

....

....

....

....

....

....

....

....

....

I DON'T WANNA MISS A THING

Do you ever see or hear about people hanging out together or at places without you? Or maybe you've seen people out somewhere seemingly amazing while you are stuck at home? Write about whether and how this makes you anxious.

....

....

....

....

....

....

....

....

NOT FEELING IT

Do you sometimes worry that someone in particular doesn't like you? Describe why you think this person might not like you, and how it makes you feel.

....

....

....

....

....

....

....

....

....

SCARED TO BE LONELY

Do you ever feel disconnected from your peer group or worry about fitting in? Do you ever think that maybe you don't have enough friends? Or that your friendships are too superficial? Write about these concerns.

....

....

....

....

....

....

....

....

WORRY DUMP!

Get it all out. Write or draw anything that is upsetting you. Visualize your anxieties and put them here. Imagine a giant trash can and toss all your anxiety-producing thoughts and worries into it!

HATERS

Have you ever been bullied or seen someone be bullied? Whether it is physical, emotional, or happens online, it is something you can't always avoid, and it can feel very traumatic. If it is happening or has happened to you, you aren't alone. Describe what happened and how you have tried to cope with it.

AWKWARD

Write about a social mistake or faux pas you think you made. It can be something you said or did IRL, or something you posted on social media. What happened? How did you feel? Why do you think it was a mistake?

....

....

....

....

....

....

....

....

ARE YOU MAD AT ME?

Do you ever worry that someone is mad at you or upset with you, but you are uncomfortable asking them about it? What makes you think they are unhappy with you?

....

....

....

....

....

....

....

SAVE THE DRAMA

Friendship drama can be superintense and create A LOT of anxiety. Describe an upsetting friend situation, past or present. In what ways did it make you feel anxious?

SORRY NOT SORRY

Disagreements can get really hot when people have very different perspectives. Write about a time that you got into an argument with someone. Did you feel misunderstood? How do you think the other person felt? How did this conflict affect your feelings of anxiety?

BLAME GAME

Write about an ongoing conflict with a specific family member (parent, caregiver, sibling, or other close relationship). How does this person currently treat you? How does that make you feel? How would you rather be treated?

TOGETHERNESS

Are there specific family experiences that you find stressful (such as holiday gatherings, vacations, or even daily meals)? Write about how you feel at these events.

_____

_____

_____

_____

_____

_____

_____

_____

_____

_____

_____

_____

_____

_____

_____

_____

_____

_____

_____

_____

_____

NOT THERE YET

Do you ever feel like everyone else is dating except you? Are you not ready yet? Or you would like to have a romantic partner but you feel it is never going to happen? Write down your feelings about this situation.

....

....

....

....

....

....

....

....

BAD ROMANCE

Dating (thinking about it, doing it) can be hugely stressful. Write about any current or past worry about dating. For example, are you using any dating apps? Are you finding them confusing to navigate?

....

....

....

....

....

....

....

I GOT A CRUSH ON YOU

Having a crush on someone can feel extremely intense in both good and bad ways. Does this make you anxious? Do you feel worried about approaching this person?

....

....

....

....

....

....

....

....

JUST A FRIEND

Do you ever worry that someone you are crushing on won't like you back? Write about a time in the past or present when feelings may not have been reciprocated. How did you feel? How did you act?

....

....

....

....

....

....

....

STUCK IN THE MIDDLE

A common but super-uncomfortable situation is when you and a buddy like the same person—or when you have to choose between two people who are romantically into you. Describe what happened, and the ways it triggered your anxiety.

....

....

....

....

....

....

....

....

HEARTLESS

Has someone ever really liked you and you had to turn them down? Did you worry about hurting that person's feelings? How did your worries affect your actions?

....

....

....

....

....

....

....

....

TOTAL REJECTION

Have you been rejected or ghosted by someone? (Know that it happens to all of us and is incredibly painful.) What was this experience like for you? Did you ultimately recover?

....

....

....

....

....

....

....

....

FRIENDS WITH BENEFITS

It can be confusing to figure out if a relationship is casual or more serious. It's hard to tell sometimes if one person is on a different page about the relationship. Write about a time you wanted more or less out of a connection.

....

....

....

....

....

....

....

....

HEARTBREAKERS GONNA BREAK

Breakups are the worst. Describe breaking up with someone or being
broken up with. Did this make you anxious? What were your specific worries?

....
....
....
....
....
....
....
....

ALL THE SINGLE . . .

If you are currently single, how do you feel about this? Happy or worried? Do you
wish you were dating someone, or not? How often do you think about this?

....
....
....
....
....
....
....
....

LOVE ON THE BRAIN

Hooking up (thinking about it, doing it) can make people feel very anxious.
Write about any current or past worries you may have had about physical intimacy
with someone.

....

....

....

....

....

....

....

....

SHAPE OF YOU

Do you worry about being attractive enough to your current or potential partner?
How do these worries affect your choices and behavior?

....

....

....

....

....

....

....

....

....

SAFE WITH ME

Do you feel concerned about going further with someone than you are comfortable with? Have you ever struggled with issues related to consent? Describe how you felt. Did the situation cause new anxieties or unease?

....

....

....

....

....

....

....

SEX EDUCATION

Do you ever worry about whether you are doing something correctly when you are being physically intimate? Do you ever feel reluctant to speak up if something isn't working for you (i.e. Do you feel like you can ask for what you want or need?) Do you worry that the other person is not feeling satisfied? How do these worries play out in your actions?

....

....

....

....

....

....

....

WORRY DUMP!

Get it all out. Write or draw anything that is upsetting you. Visualize your anxieties and put them here. Imagine a giant trash can and toss all your anxiety-producing thoughts and worries into it!

IDENTITY CRISIS

Do you ever worry that an aspect of your identity, such as race, gender, or sexuality, will not be accepted by others or cause people to discriminate against you? These are serious and legitimate concerns. Describe your worries in detail.

TEXT ME

Write (but don't send!) a text, DM, or email to a friend with thoughts you wish you could share but have been afraid to. What would you say if there were no consequences?

. . .

SECRETS

Every person has some feelings about themselves that they are afraid to examine too deeply. Sometimes getting close to these thoughts can produce very anxious feelings, but it's safe to write them here.

My deepest, darkest thoughts about myself:

o

o

o

o

o

BEAUTY AND A BEAT

It is not possible to be human without being self-conscious! Which aspects of your body (i.e. shape, weight, height, hair, muscularity, other) do you wish you could change? Which ones do you like?

What I like:

....

....

....

....

Why:

....

....

....

....

What I don't like:

....

....

....

....

Why:

....

....

....

....

INNER CRITIC

We all have an inner critic that likes to throw shade. We can be really hard on ourselves as a result! What does your inner critic say about you? List several criticisms you have about yourself.

-

-

-

-

-

ALMOST IS NEVER ENOUGH

Do you try to achieve perfection in certain areas? Write about any really high
standard(s) you may have for yourself. How do you feel when you examine these
expectations? Do you feel you are falling short?

SCHOOL DAZE

School is stressful! List any worries you are having about exams or grades or assignments. If you're finished with school, try to remember what it was like, and write about any anxieties you experienced around your studies.

SUBJECT/ASSIGNMENT	CONCERN

TOTAL ANTICIPATION

Do you worry about the first day of something, like the first day of school, college, or work? What feelings are you having when you think about going? Describe your physical and mental state when you think about entering this situation.

UNDER PRESSURE

Being called upon in class, having to give a presentation at work, even reading aloud—any kind of public speaking can make you feel overwhelmed with anxiety. Write about a time when you had to speak or perform in public. Describe your physical and mental state, and how you felt afterward. What happens when you think about doing it again?

PARTY JITTERS

Social events—a date, a party, or prom, even a casual group brunch—can bring on worried feelings, depending on who's attending, your state of mind, and other factors. What anxious feelings might come up when you're thinking about attending a social event?

ALL-STAR

Athletic pursuits can be extremely anxiety-producing, whether you are trying out for a team, playing an important game, or even just participating in a casual, occasional way. Write about what this is like for you.

....

....

....

....

....

....

....

I AM NOT THROWING AWAY MY SHOT

Everyone worries about being talented enough at the things they enjoy doing, whether it is music, theater, chess, art, poetry, knitting, or what have you. What are some of the worries that diminish the pleasure you take in doing something you like and/or something you are talented at?

....

....

....

....

....

....

....

ACHIEVE, BELIEVE

Write about something you hope to achieve in your life that you are concerned is going to be difficult or may not happen (like getting into college, finding a good job, or falling in love).

GOAL	WORRIES

WORK, WORK, WORK

Work is stressful! Even a part-time gig produces stress, whether it's from dealing with your boss, your performance, your coworkers, your salary, or your commute.

List some job-related concerns.

○

○

○

○

○

MONEY ON MY MIND

Money can be among of the most stressful aspects of our lives. Do you worry about having enough money? How do you feel about saving money? Do you worry about how you spend it or earning enough? Write about your money worries.

....

....

....

....

....

....

....

....

....

....

....

....

....

....

....

....

....

....

....

....

....

....

....

WORRIED SICK

What worries do you have about your health?

SYMPTOM	WHAT COULD HAPPEN?

Do you worry about any other people's health, such as a loved one? Write down all your worries.

PERSON	WHAT COULD HAPPEN?

AS THE WORLD TURNS

The world around us can be so hectic! Some people cope by ignoring it and others by obsessing over it. How do you cope with concerns about current events? Pick a few things to write about.

EVENT	HOW IT MAKES ME FEEL

RING THE ALARM

Do you ever feel concerned for your own personal safety? Do you worry about robbers or being robbed, mugged, or physically assaulted? (PS If you have an imminent concern about this, you really need to tell someone!!)

INDEPENDENCE DAY

Are there any particular tasks (like paying bills, driving, flying) that you feel worried about doing on your own? Write about situations where you worry about being independent or self-sufficient.

....

....

....

....

....

....

....

....

SEPARATION ANXIETY

Do you worry about something bad happening to anyone in your family? Or to your pets? Write about any safety concerns you have for people or animals that you care about. Do you feel anxious when you are not with loved ones or worried about being away from them?

....

....

....

....

....

....

....

INNER ACTIVIST

Is there a cause you are passionate about but that stresses you out? Do you worry about this issue or feel you aren't doing enough?

....

....

....

....

....

....

....

....

....

CONFIDENT

Write about a famous figure or person you admire who is simply badass. Do you wish you could be more like them? What would you like to do?

....

....

....

....

....

....

....

....

....

DON'T WORRY, BE HAPPY

If you could be sure you'd never experience anxiety again, is there anything you would do differently in your life? Are there things you would like to do that you feel you cannot do now? What would your life be like if you had absolutely no worries?

FIVE-YEAR PLAN

Envision yourself in five years. Where do you want to be and what do you want to be doing? (You don't have to be specific.) Did your anxiety help you get there?

PART II

WHAT CAN YOU DO ABOUT IT?

**IDENTIFY AND CHALLENGE
YOUR ANXIOUS THOUGHT PATTERNS
THAT ARE CREATING STRESS.**

I HOPE YOU have discovered that venting makes you feel better! Putting your anxious feelings into words helps your brain shift gears from fretful to thoughtful, and that change alone can be calming. This next section will enable you to take this process one step further by introducing strategies that you can use to help alleviate your worries. These proven techniques are widely used in cognitive behavioral therapy (CBT) and have helped millions of worriers feel considerably less anxious and more at ease.

THE WORRY TRIANGLE

One of the most effective ways to challenge anxiety is to break down worries into smaller pieces that you can tackle which will lessen their power. Any emotion you have (either positive or negative, like happiness or worry) can be broken down into three components:

1. The **thought** that brings on the feeling

2. The **feeling** itself (including any physical sensations that accompany this emotion)

3. The **action** (or inaction) that you take when you experience this thought and this feeling

One incredibly useful way to look at anxiety is as a subtle and powerful trifecta of worry thoughts + worry feelings + worry actions. After all, breaking things down makes them much easier to tackle. Therapists call this the worry triangle. Here are a couple of examples of how it plays out:

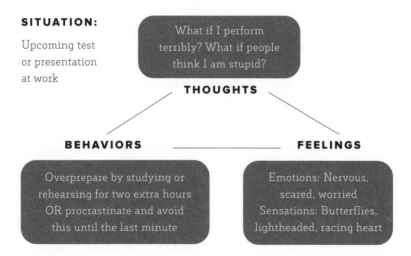

SITUATION:

Upcoming test
or presentation
at work

What if I perform terribly? What if people think I am stupid?

THOUGHTS

BEHAVIORS

Overprepare by studying or rehearsing for two extra hours OR procrastinate and avoid this until the last minute

FEELINGS

Emotions: Nervous, scared, worried
Sensations: Butterflies, lightheaded, racing heart

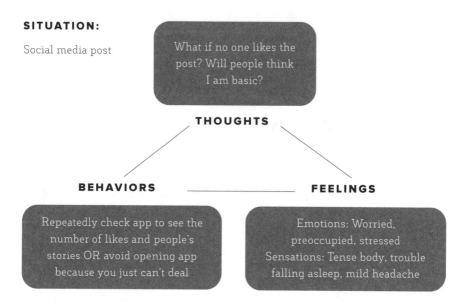

SITUATION:

Social media post

What if no one likes the post? Will people think I am basic?

THOUGHTS

BEHAVIORS

Repeatedly check app to see the number of likes and people's stories OR avoid opening app because you just can't deal

FEELINGS

Emotions: Worried, preoccupied, stressed
Sensations: Tense body, trouble falling asleep, mild headache

As you can see, anxiety forms a cycle: an anxious thought typically leads to an anxious emotion, which then causes us to either avoid a situation that worries us *or* to take some sort of extra safety action (like texting someone repeatedly for reassurance about something or overstudying for a test). These "worry behaviors" (avoidance, overcompensation) then inadvertently make the anxiety more intense because you don't get a chance to disprove your concern. Worry behaviors tend to subtly confirm the worry thoughts we are having about that situation, which in turn intensifies our anxious feelings, creating a problematic cycle of worry.

Worry behaviors (a.k.a. "safety behaviors") can be really subtle, so watch out for them! Checking your work repeatedly, reassurance seeking, doomscrolling, internet rabbit holes, cyberstalking, people-pleasing, and planning far in advance are all examples. You may think these behaviors will reduce your worry but in fact they will make it worse.

The good news is that you can break this cycle. Breaking the worry into these three parts helps us attack each component separately with specific strategies tailored to each part. Get started by practicing breaking down some of your top worries into these three components (thought, feeling, and action), and then you can build examples of your own worry triangles. We'll then discuss how to interrupt the cycle at each stage—thoughts, feelings, and behaviors.

WORRY TRIANGLE PRACTICE

Write down a recent situation that made you feel worried (feel free to use one of the examples here, or a new one). What was the specific worry that you had? Write down the emotion you felt (nervous, stressed, anxious) as well as any physical sensations (racing heart, sweatiness, butterflies). Lastly, write down what you did or didn't do when you had this worry (sent unnecessary email, canceled plans).

SITUATION:

THOUGHTS

BEHAVIORS _____ FEELINGS

AUTOMATIC NEGATIVE THOUGHTS (ANTS)

Worry is often *triggered* (set off) by a negative thought, idea, or interpretation of a given situation. Often, these thoughts are automatic—they just pop into your head, and you instantly accept them as accurate without really examining them. Understanding that our minds may have gotten into the habit of generating negative thoughts that we may not even be aware of (but that cause anxiety) can be incredibly helpful. Therapists actually refer to these as ANTs (automatic negative thoughts).

For example, you might be worried about an upcoming test, and your ANTs unfold something like this: "I am worried that I may get a C on my chem final, which will look horrible on my report card. No decent college or university will accept me and I will never be able to get into medical school." Or "I said something stupid in that meeting. Now my boss will lose confidence in me, and I will get a bad review and lose my job."

If you pay attention to your ANTs and begin noticing and identifying them, you can start to see how they might be causing you anxiety—and learn to disarm them. In this section, you're going to practice identifying and unpacking your ANTs so you can see how your thoughts might be making your situation seem much worse than it is.

THINKING OUT LOUD

Pick a worry that has been bothering you—you can choose one that you've already written about or select a fresh one. Be really specific. Now answer the following questions:

Worry: _____

_____

What am I saying to myself right now?

....

....

What story am I telling myself about this situation?

....

....

What specifically am I afraid of?

....

....

**What is the worst possible outcome that could happen
in this situation?**

....

....

**Of all the worries going on in my head now, which one is
trending the most?**

....

....

THINKING TRAPS

Now that you have identified one or more automatic negative thoughts, the next step is to figure out whether this thought makes sense or whether it might be a thinking trap. In order to manage worry, it can be incredibly helpful to identify patterns of thinking that contribute to anxious feelings and examine whether they might be flawed or unrealistic. Learning to identify and/or counter these "thinking traps" can bring great relief from anxiety and worry. A **thinking trap** is a way of seeing things that is often negative and unrealistic—a distortion of reality. How does this happen? When we worry, there is usually an element to the worry that is at least slightly irrational. Often, we jump to conclusions about something without having any evidence for it. There are lots of thinking traps that our worries fall into every day without us realizing it. Frequently, when I discuss different types of thinking traps with my anxious patients, they tell me that they recognize ALL of them. This is because these thinking styles are universal—everyone engages in these types of thinking patterns from time to time, especially if you have anxiety. Further, often a particular worry can fall into multiple traps.

In this section, we are going to practice recognizing some of the most common thinking traps and countering them with more realistic thoughts.

MIND READING

Assuming you know what other people are thinking about you or a particular situation—such as somebody's opinion of you or reasons someone is behaving a certain way toward you—even though you cannot read minds and have no actual evidence or proof about what anyone thinks. (And, to be honest, most people are thinking about themselves most of the time, not about you!)

- "That girl in my poetry class thinks I am so cringey."
- "Everyone is staring at my pimple."
- "She had an angry look on her face and is obviously mad at me."

Write down some examples of mind reading that you have engaged in:

JUMPING TO CONCLUSIONS

Immediately arriving at a conclusion about a situation without thinking it through or without considering all the relevant information about a situation.

- "I sneezed three times; I must have caught a terrible virus."
- "The dog didn't come to the door to greet me; she must have run away!"
- "I didn't get a text back. My friend isn't speaking to me anymore."

Write down some conclusions you have jumped to:

....

....

....

....

....

....

....

....

....

....

....

....

....

....

....

....

....

....

NEGATIVE FORECASTING

Making predictions about the future even though you don't have a crystal ball. Sometimes this takes the form of "what-ifs." Typically you decide that something bad (versus something good) is definitely going to happen.

- "There is no way I am going to get this job."
- "My parents had an argument. I'm pretty sure they're going to get a divorce."
- "What if I get a bad grade on this test and my GPA is destroyed?"

Write down some negative forecasts you have about events in your life:

ALL—OR—NOTHING THINKING

Thinking in black-and-white terms. A clue that you're doing this is use of the words "always" or "never."

- "No one will ever fall in love with me."
- "Why do bad things always happen to me?"
- "My butt always looks fat in jeans."
- "Why can't I ever have fun at parties?"

Write down your own all-or-nothings.

FEELINGS AS FACTS

Deciding that because you have a strong feeling about something or have come to a specific conclusion about a situation, these feelings must reflect the absolute truth. Therapists also call this emotional reasoning (using emotions as proof).

- "I have a strong feeling she is mad at me, so she must be mad at me."

- "I'm very scared of flying, so it must be dangerous."

- "My heart is pounding; therefore, if I give this speech, I will pass out."

Write down examples of confusing your feelings with facts:

PERSONALIZING

Making it all about you; concluding that whenever something less than ideal happens, it is related to some imagined flaw or defect that you feel that you have—when in fact the situation may have absolutely nothing, or very little, to do with you.

- "My crush didn't ask me to the dance because I am not attractive enough."
- "Our team didn't make the playoffs because of my bad performance."
- "My partner broke up with me because my personality sucks."

Write down your versions of personalizing:

....

....

....

....

....

....

....

....

....

....

....

....

....

....

....

....

JUDGING AND LABELING

Having negative beliefs or ideas about yourself that lead you to calling yourself insulting names.

- "I am stupid."

- "I suck."

- "I am a bad person."

Write down negative beliefs you've held or continue to hold about yourself:

UNFAIR COMPARISONS

Deciding that another person or people are much better than you at something (or everything!) and then feeling badly about your own experience by comparison. Typically the comparison isn't really fair because you may not have the whole story.

- "Everyone else on this team is a better runner than me."
- "She looks so hot in that Insta post; her life must be perfect."
- "My friends go out on dates almost every night. Why not me?"
- "My colleagues are getting promoted ahead of me, and I am never going to catch up."

Write down some examples of unfair comparisons you've applied to yourself:

IGNORING THE POSITIVE

Filtering out or discounting positive things about yourself or a situation and/or zooming in on the negative.

- "I did well on the test, but I can't stop thinking about the one answer I got wrong."
- "We won the game, but I totally screwed up that pass."
- "My crush wasn't at the party, so the night was a total loss."

Write down some times you have focused on the negative instead of the positive:

....

....

....

....

....

....

....

....

....

....

....

....

....

....

....

....

....

MINIMIZING

Deciding that something good doesn't matter.

- "That is what I am supposed to do, so it doesn't count."
- "That person was only complimenting me to be nice."
- "My accomplishments don't matter because I am so unhappy."

Give some examples of you minimizing or downplaying something about yourself or a situation that is good:

SHOULD STATEMENTS

Deciding that you should or must do something to be okay, or that things absolutely have to be a certain way or else they are terrible.

- "I should always be the top student in class."
- "I shouldn't have eaten any dessert."
- "I should never feel sad."

Write down some should statements that you have used:

....

....

....

....

....

....

....

....

....

....

....

....

....

....

....

....

....

....

BLOWING THINGS UP

Concluding that something relatively minor either is a big problem or totally the end of the world. After all, anxiety often leads us to believe that everything is an absolute emergency.

- "I got a stain on my shirt—it is completely destroyed and I might as well throw it out."

- "I have to miss the biggest party of the season. My life is basically over!"

- "I didn't get what I wanted for my birthday, and now the whole day is ruined."

Give some examples of when you have blown things out of proportion:

....

....

....

....

....

....

....

....

....

....

....

....

....

....

....

....

....

SELF—BLAMING

Concluding that something is most definitely, without a doubt, your fault.

- "If I had been a cooler person, they would not have ghosted me."
- "My parents broke up because of me."
- "It is my fault that this friendship ended."

Give some examples of times when you've unfairly put the blame all on yourself:

....

....

....

....

....

....

....

....

....

....

....

....

....

....

....

....

....

....

GUILT–TRIPPING

Obsessing over the idea that you did something wrong or let someone down and feeling guilt-stricken over it (even if you didn't actually do anything that bad or intend for a particular outcome to happen).

- "I am a terrible friend because I didn't text her back right away when she was upset."

- "I said something mean; I'm a bad person."

- "I am so selfish. I know I should have spent time with my mom, but I wanted to hang out with my friends instead."

Think of some instances when you have guilt-tripped yourself into feeling anxious:

....

....

....

....

....

....

....

....

....

....

....

....

....

....

SETTING THE BAR TOO HIGH

The perfectionistic and self-defeating tendency to set unrealistic expectations for yourself (and sometimes others, but mainly yourself) that are difficult, if not impossible, to reach.

- "I absolutely must get a perfect score on my SATs."
- "Every post has to get 100 likes or I'm a failure."
- "I should never experience disappointment or rejection."

In what ways have you set your bar too high?

SPOTLIGHTING

Believing that you are different from everyone else in a negative way—
as if a spotlight of misfortune is shining on you alone.

- "I am the only one who is having this problem."

- "No one else has social anxiety except me."

- "Other people seem to have it completely together, but I am always a hot mess."

Write down some examples of when you have thought of yourself in a spotlighting way:

....

....

....

....

....

....

....

....

....

....

....

....

....

....

....

....

....

....

LOOK OUT FOR COMMON THINKING TRAPS

There are many thinking traps, but most of our worries tend to fall into the same ones over and over. Further, it is not uncommon for a particular worry thought to fall into more than one trap (i.e. worrying about getting sick can be an example of jumping to conclusions, negative forecasting, and all-or-nothing thinking.) It can be helpful to identify which ones are most habitual for you so you can learn to recognize and look out for them.

Circle up to five of the thinking traps that your worries most frequently fall into:

Jumping to
conclusions

Negative
forecasting

Mind
reading

Feelings
as facts

All-or-nothing
thinking

Personalizing

Self-blaming

Unfair
comparisons

Judging and
labeling

Should
statements

Ignoring
the positive

Blowing
things up

Setting the
bar too high

Minimizing

Spotlighting

Guilt-tripping

ANXIOUS THINKING PATTERNS

If it feels too hard to keep track of all the different thinking traps your worry can fall into, you can instead focus on the two *most common* types of anxious thinking that people experience. While doing the thinking trap exercises, you may have noticed that your worries tend to fall into two broad categories:

- PROBABILITY OVERESTIMATION: Overestimating the likelihood of something (almost always very bad) happening.

- CATASTROPHIZING: Deciding that if this outcome were in fact to occur, it would be a complete and total disaster from which you would not be able to recover.

These two prominent thinking traps essentially throw you into the worry cycle. If you overestimate the probability of danger and underestimate your ability to cope, it's no wonder you feel anxious!

For example, let's say you did not get a response to a text you sent, and you are 100 percent convinced that your friend now hates you, which is going to be an utter disaster that will destroy your social life. In reality, it is pretty unlikely (more like less than 2 percent) that your friend despises you, and in the off chance they are actually mad, there will be ways to fix it. You could apologize, give this person space until it blows over, or accept the consequences, move on, and focus on other relationships. It might suck a little bit, but you *can* cope.

FIGHT BACK!

Anxiety plays tricks on us! Now that you have an understanding of thinking traps, you are ready to start actually challenging the distorted thoughts and faulty interpretations (a.k.a. automatic negative thoughts, or ANTs) that are making you feel anxious. Remember, worried thoughts lead to worried feelings. If you want to stop feeling worried, you need to change your interpretation of a given situation by reframing and shifting your perspective. Effectively, you need to change your mind!

In this section, you will learn to ask yourself **strategic questions** to challenge and dilute the power of your worry thoughts, and then you will answer those questions in a calm and balanced way. We will refer to these answers as reasonable responses (RRs.)

It can be helpful to think of yourself as a lawyer who is putting your worry thoughts on trial and exploring whether there is evidence to support or refute them. I encourage you to employ this strategy not just a couple of times, but over and over—for every single worry you have. It only takes a few seconds of critical thinking and has a big payoff! You can practice on paper or inside your head. Over time, it will become second nature and you will get in the habit of:

- identifying your ANT about a situation,
- selecting a thinking trap it could fall into,
- arguing with it by asking questions,
- answering those questions with RRs, and
- feeling relieved!

Remember, you do not have to be fully convinced of every counterargument to your worries for these skills to work. You *do* have to fully entertain the notion that there could be another reasonable way to think about the situation. The key to anxiety management is thinking flexibly, not rigidly!

WORST-CASE SCENARIO

Think about a situation that you are worried about and answer the questions below.

Situation:

....

....

....

....

Worst thing I think could happen:

....

....

....

....

How realistic is this worst-case scenario?

....

....

....

....

What is a more realistic outcome?

....

....

....

....

STATISTICS ARE ON YOUR SIDE

Statistically speaking, worst-case scenarios are the least likely to occur. Just because something is *possible* does not make it *probable*. Think about the worst-case scenario you just identified and distinguish between it being merely possible to actually likely. Is this feared scenario 100 percent likely? Or closer to 1 or 2 percent likely?

Describe the situation and the true likelihood of your feared outcome occurring.

NOT SO BAD

If the worst did happen, how bad would it *really* be? Could you deal with it?
(Note: This question doesn't work in cases of death or true disaster, so save it for
less catastrophic worries.) For example, if your dog ate your homework, it would
completely suck, but you could always start over and do it again even if you didn't
want to. List some things you could do to handle it.

Adverse situation or outcome:

....

....

....

How I could deal with it:

....

....

....

Adverse situation or outcome:

....

....

....

How I could deal with it:

....

....

....

LAWYER UP

Choose the top worry on your mind right now. Do you have any actual evidence or proof that it is going to happen? (It is okay to admit that you don't!) Further, can you think of any counterevidence that suggests your worry probably won't happen or will turn out okay? (For example, your friend tends to be terrible at returning texts promptly.)

Describe any evidence or counterevidence here.

YOU BE THE JUDGE

If you do have evidence that supports your worry, how reliable is that evidence? Do you have reasons to doubt this evidence? Would it be upheld in court or thrown out? (For example, if your "evidence" is from the internet.)

Write your evidence here and comment on its reliability.

ANTICIPATION VS. REALITY

Anticipation is often the worst part of worry—we may spend hours before the onset of an event feeling convinced that it is going to turn out poorly.

Write about some calamity or stressful outcome that you were worried was going to happen within the past year. What actually happened? Was it nearly as bad as you thought it was going to be?

ALTERNATIVE OUTCOMES

Think about something in your life that you worry is going to turn out badly.
Consider past experience. What else could happen? What is another, more likely
outcome for this situation?

Write it all out here.

TELL A FRIEND

We can't always be objective about our own worries, but if a friend approaches us for advice, there is a sudden shift. Pretend a close friend has approached you with one of your personal worries. What comforting things would you tell a friend about this situation? Or ask yourself, "How would someone else (who isn't me) think about this?"

Describe what you might say.

GOOD ADVICE

What advice would a therapist, friend, or mentor give you about this situation? In the past, when you have been worried about something, what comforting advice were you given?

Write it here.

....

....

....

....

....

....

....

....

....

....

....

....

....

....

....

....

....

....

....

....

....

....

....

....

....

FACTS!

Sometimes when we have worries, we assume these negative thoughts are the absolute truth. However, worries are just thoughts—more similar to opinions than facts. (For example, a thought that red is the best color or that it is totally going to rain tomorrow.) Are your thoughts absolute reflections of reality? List a worry or two that are more likely your subjective opinion versus factual truth.

0

0

0

0

0

0

0

0

0

FAKE NEWS

Similarly, just because someone else says something does not make it automatically true. Do you very typically believe that someone else's opinion equals the objective truth? Are you basing a worry on something you heard? Is that person a reliable source? Could that person be saying something due a personal issue?

Give an example of something someone said recently (i.e. something mean or negative or worrisome) that might not be completely true:

....

....

....

....

....

....

....

....

....

....

....

....

....

....

....

....

....

ALL THE FEELS

Think about something worrying you. Are you basing your concern entirely on your feelings about the situation? Even though your feelings are very strong, that does not mean they reflect reality. Are your emotions the same as hard evidence? Example: You *feel* anxious, so you assume the anxiety is justified. Or you have a feeling that your partner might be cheating on you—does that mean it's true?

List some of your own examples, or describe a time when you went down the path of emotional reasoning. Remember, feelings are not facts!

POSER

Pretend your anxiety is a fake Instagram account. Your anxious thoughts seem undeniably accurate to you and you may be tempted to treat them as the real thing—but the "posts" are fake and you'd do best to unfollow them. They are, at minimum, well out of proportion to reality.

Share some of your most fantastical worries that are definitely not true.

Example: The pain you felt in your side when you ran to catch the bus means that you have a deadly disease and won't live to see thirty.

Then write reasons why they are unlikely to be true. (For example, you have had pains before and did not die.)

....

....

....

....

....

....

....

....

....

....

....

....

....

....

....

....

BLAST FROM THE PAST

Think about a concern you are currently having. In a similar situation in the past, how did it ultimately get resolved or work out?

Write down some past experiences similar to the current one that turned out okay.

YOU'VE GOT THIS

In the past, if something stressful happened, were you able to handle it? Could you draw on those resources again?

Explain how you worked it out.

CRYSTAL BALL

Sometimes a previous bad experience makes us fearful or fully convinced that this thing is going to keep happening. But history does not necessarily repeat itself—just because something happened one time does not mean it is going to happen again.

Write about a worry you have. Do you know with absolute certainty that it is going to happen again? Describe what could happen differently:

WOULDA SHOULDA COULDA

Think of a time you were convinced you should or should not have done something. Then answer the following questions: Who or what says that you have to do something that way? Why? And was it really that bad? If YOU are the person telling yourself that you "should" or "should not" have done that or that you "should" or "should not" do something in the present moment, are you absolutely right?

Below, list as many of your "should" statements as possible. Examples: "I should not have said that." "I should always only say nice things." Decide whether they are correct. Place a check mark next to any that are truly accurate and an X next to the ones that you could think differently about.

NO FAULT

Think about a time you blamed yourself. Are you absolutely certain that this situation was your fault?

Example: You are sure that your date ended poorly because you said something stupid. Is it possible, however, that your date might be socially awkward? Or was having a bad day? List some other circumstances that could have contributed to this problem.

Situation: ....

....

....

What I did or didn't do that I think caused a bad outcome: ....

....

....

Other reasons that could account for the way things turned out: ....

....

....

Situation: ....

....

....

What I did or didn't do that I think caused a bad outcome: ....

....

....

Other reasons that could account for the way things turned out: ....

....

....

NOT GUILTY

The last time you felt guilty about something, did you actually do anything wrong? Is the guilt justified? Was whatever you did so bad? Did you intend for it to happen? Are you allowed to make mistakes? Is whatever it is something that will blow over? Or is there something you can do to make amends?

Sometimes circumstances are unforeseeable, and sometimes we play a small role in something but did not intend for it to turn out a certain way. Be careful of being too hard on yourself.

List things you feel guilty about below, and decide whether the guilt is really justified. If it is (unlikely), then describe what you can do to amend the situation.

THINGS I FEEL GUILTY ABOUT	JUSTIFIED?	OPTIONS FOR MAKING IT BETTER

EXAGGERATIONS

Are you blowing a situation out of proportion, and making it a bigger deal than it actually is? If _____ happens, is it actually going to be that bad? Does so-and-so's opinion really matter so much? Is _____ truly the end of the world?

List some worries you have and identify which parts of the situation may be exaggerated by your anxiety. What is the more realistic view?

TIME CAPSULE

Consider one of your worries in the grand scheme of things.
What difference will this make tomorrow, next week, next year?

List any future repercussions (if any) you think are truly likely:

- ○

- ○

- ○

- ○

- ○

SILVER LININGS PLAYBOOK

Difficult experiences build character and resilience. TBH, we often have to go through hard things in order to grow and move forward in life. Is there any conceivable way to look at a worrisome situation positively? For example, is it possible that something good could come out of it or that you could learn something from it?

Write down a few ways to look at one of your top anxiety-producing situations positively:

WHY WORRY?

You've identified a worry and concluded that it is a realistic concern. (Example: A family member is ill). However, is remaining preoccupied with the problem productive or likely to just make you feel worse?

Describe a realistic worry that you have, and write about whether dwelling on it is truly going to be helpful:

....

....

....

....

....

....

....

....

....

....

....

....

....

....

....

....

....

....

....

....

....

....

SAVE YOUR TEARS

Often, insecurity gets the better of us and we feel absolutely convinced that others think negative things about us (despite the fact that most people are not as judgmental as we assume they are). When you feel convinced that someone is judging you, it is important to ask the following questions: Do I know for certain that _____ thinks this about me? Can I read minds? Is it possible they are not thinking about me at all or are only thinking about themselves? Perhaps they are even thinking something neutral or positive about me?

Describe a recent time that you were convinced someone thought poorly of you or thought something insulting or negative about you. What was your reasoning? Did you have any hard evidence of this? Can you supply an alternative explanation?

ACCURATE SELF-ASSESSMENT

Often, we aren't the best judge of ourselves and we are way too hard on ourselves. In the first column, list some negative things you routinely say or think about yourself.

In the next column, explain how accurate or fair your assessment really is.

NEGATIVE QUALITY	HOW TRUE OR FALSE IS IT, REALLY?

PERFECT ILLUSION

Think about someone whose social media (or general persona) has left you feeling that their life is perfect compared to yours. Now write an alternative, more realistic backstory for that person. Is it possible that this person experiences hardship? What could the social media posts (or the person's appearance) be leaving out? Next, write about aspects of your own life that are actually pretty good (or at least not so bad). If someone else has some success, does that mean your life is terrible?

Perfect Person's persona: (What seems perfect about this person?)

....

....

....

....

....

Perfect Person's backstory: (What else could be going on?)

....

....

....

....

....

My Pretty Good story: (What is going well in my life?)

....

....

....

....

....

....

IT'S NOT PERSONAL

Think of a comment or situation that you took personally and that made you feel defensive or badly about yourself or that you assumed was your fault. Now imagine a version where it is not all about you. (It is almost always not actually about you!)

Write down another explanation for what happened.

(For example, is the other person projecting something or going through something that you may not be aware of? Maybe they're just brusque or abrasive or having a hard day.)

NOT JUST YOU

Think of a problem that you believe no one else has to deal with. Are you really the only one with this problem? Can you think of some other people (they can be real or fictional) who might have dealt with similar feelings or situations?

Write down who these people are and/or how you think they might have handled it.

Problem:

....

....

Who else has it?

....

....

How do they deal?

....

....

If you have family members or friends who you think might understand your anxieties or hardships or who have been through similar things, consider asking them how they have handled it. Knowing that others have experienced anxious feelings and intense stress can help you feel less alone and more capable.

Write down any takeaways you learn from them.

-
-
-
-
-

PART III

HOW CAN YOU OVERCOME WORRY?

**UNCOVER KEY WORRY THEMES
AND LEARN WAYS TO COMPLETELY
SHIFT YOUR PERSPECTIVE.**

AS WE LEARNED in Part II, one of the main goals of worry management is to change your patterns of anxious thinking. You are learning how to replace your ANTs and the feelings and behaviors that arise from them with more reasonable and balanced ideas that will help you feel calm. Some of the terms that therapists use to describe these healthier thoughts are reasonable responses, coping statements, cheerleading statements, or positive self-talk.

Coping statements counter your worries by presenting a perspective switch to break you out of your worry cycle. They tend to be upbeat and optimistic—but not foolishly positive. Managing anxiety doesn't involve rainbows and unicorns; it involves shifting our thinking to a more balanced, reasonable, or neutral place, which in turn helps us feel calmer and more at ease. Using these statements is a fantastic shortcut when you do not have time to go through the steps of identifying thinking traps and challenging specific worries. They allow you to cut to the chase and feel better very quickly! In fact, using coping statements is a key strategy for managing anxiety. Some people find it helpful to put their favorites on index cards or in their phone, or you can bank them away in your memory to review when you are having a tough moment.

In this section, you will engage in thought exercises to help you shift your perspective on your worries. You will review sample coping statements related to these themes and can come up with your own if you'd like!

#COPINGSTATEMENTS

Here are some examples of #copingstatements that allow you to modify what your anxious brain is saying to you and change the way you think. Read them slowly, one at a time, and see which ones have a calming effect on you:

- This is rough, but I can handle it.
- It's going to be okay. I've got this.
- I am not my anxiety. I am separate from my emotions.
- Difficult situations are usually temporary. This will blow over.
- I will not feel this way forever.
- Asking for help is a sign of strength, not a sign of weakness.
- Thinking something doesn't make it true.
- I rule—I am staying in the situation even though it is hard.
- Things are going to get better and easier over time.

In this section, you will practice coming up with your own #copingstatements to help counter your worries and brighten your mood. A good coping statement is realistic and shifts focus from the content of your worry to an alternative way to look at a situation or problem you are facing. Think about what you would tell a friend who was worried or upset!

Come up with five effective coping statements and write them here:

....

....

....

....

....

....

....

....

TALKING BACK TO WORRY

Coping statements can be used successfully to talk back to your worry. It can be helpful to think of your worry as email spam or fake news that is being flooded into your inbox (by your anxious brain) to trip you up. It is okay to be pissed about this. After all, worry is living rent-free inside your head, which is unbelievably annoying! A good strategy is to think of your worry as a separate entity and tell it to scram and stop bothering you. Essentially, you want to unsubscribe from your worry by talking back to it. For example, tell your worry that it is getting canceled. It can be helpful to give your worry a name (e.g. Harvey).

An important thing to remember is that it is not effective to suppress or ghost your worry thoughts (thought suppression never works), but it *is* helpful to remember that your worry thoughts are *just thoughts*. You can acknowledge their existence, and then tell them to leave you alone. Imagine some angry statements you would like to say to your worry, while thinking about how worry has deeply inconvenienced you or messed up your life.

Review the examples below, and then come up with your own:

Harvey, you are not welcome in my brain. Scram!!

I do not appreciate having worry dumped into my head—go bother someone else!

I did not sign up for these worry emails—delete and unsubscribe!

Bye, Felicia . . .

....

....

....

....

....

....

....

....

UNCERTAINTY

"The unknown stresses me out," is something my clients tell me all the time. One of the hardest things to handle in life is its unpredictability—we can never truly know what is going to happen next. The future, after all, is TBD (unfortunately, even our good friends Alexa and Siri can't predict it).

While no one really enjoys uncertainty, and fear of the unknown is something virtually every human being feels, research shows that people with anxiety REALLY do not like it. We strongly prefer to plan ahead. In the absence of certainty, we struggle and feel uncomfortable. In fact, when we feel worried about something, it typically involves a situation with some element of uncertainty. For example, not knowing what you are going to do this weekend or what kind of job you are going to get are instances where uncertainty can be stressful (but unavoidable).

Often, when people react to uncertainty, they assume that the absence of information automatically means something bad is going to happen. This biased negative expectancy increases feelings of anxiety and stress.

Write about your typical reaction to uncertainty. Identify and describe a recent time you worried about something where you did not know how it was going to turn out. How does uncertainty make you feel, emotionally and physically? What don't you like about it?

EMBRACING UNCERTAINTY

Just because we do not know what is going to happen does *not* mean that bad things are going to happen. The absence of certainty does not equal doom! Uncertainty is not equivalent to disaster; it simply means anything can happen and not necessarily bad things. After all, most of the time, things turn out completely fine.

The key to being able to tolerate uncertainty is to embrace it fully. After all, there is literally nothing we can do about uncertainty except sit with it—it is a frequent and inevitable part of life and we can't plan everything. You almost need to "friend" uncertainty—or at the very least, try to be okay with it and try to be flexible. One of the ways to do this is to try to mindfully stay in the present moment, instead of fretting about the future.

Imagine that you were completely, 100 percent okay with uncertainty being a part of your life. Envision yourself radically embracing the fact that you simply can't predict the outcome of events and this is absolutely fine. Remind yourself that not knowing the outcome doesn't mean it will turn out badly (it could turn out completely fine, and most likely will).

Think about a situation with an unknown outcome. Next, imagine being cool as a cucumber about it. How amazing would that feel? Do you know for certain that it is going to turn out a certain way? Further, can you think of any positive aspects about not knowing what the future holds?

Read through these statements, then come up with some of your own:

Uncertainty is hard, but I can handle it.

Just because I don't know what is going to happen does *not* mean something bad is going to happen.

I love to plan—but sometimes I just have to go with the flow.

Not knowing the future is kind of cool. Life is full of surprises!

People appreciate it when other people are flexible!

....

....

....

....

CONTROL

It can be seductive to believe that if you worry about something for long enough, you can somehow influence or improve the outcome. Yet this is simply not true. Attempting to control anything or anyone (including your own thoughts) is a futile exercise and often actually makes your anxiety worse. Further, worrying itself never changes the way things turn out. It just makes us stressed.

An alternative to control is psychological flexibility—the willingness to accept that you simply cannot foresee or determine what happens in life and that is okay. This does not mean just throwing your hands in the air and giving up! It means rolling with the punches and understanding that if things fall apart from time to time, that is completely normal and acceptable.

It also means knowing that while you cannot control other people, you do have some control over yourself. You can try to be a good friend and a good person. You can use coping strategies when you feel worried or upset. You can't guarantee that you will perform perfectly under pressure, but you can study or practice (in a reasonable way—don't overdo it!) for such situations. It can be really helpful to make that distinction. Knowing what you can and cannot control is an essential part of dealing with the ups and downs of life.

What are some things in your life that you would really like to have control over but understand that you can't? Imagine what you think might happen if you let go of the attempt to control them. Would that be freeing?

List some things about yourself and your actions that you believe you *can* control:

....

....

....

....

....

....

....

....

LET IT GO!

Accepting your lack of control over events and other people can be liberating. Knowing that your worries have no effect on the outcome of any situation can free you to focus those urges on the aspects of your life and behavior that you truly can have an impact on. This in turn can make you feel less uncomfortable with the things that remain out of your control. It can also help reduce your anxiety—since trying to control (or overcontrol) too many things notoriously elevates stress levels—which is the last thing you want!

Read through and sit for a moment with each statement. Can you think of additional #copingstatements to add to help you resist the urge to exert control?

Worrying does not enable me to change the outcome of events.

Not everything can work out all the time. I am okay with that.

I am letting go of _____.

I will not waste time trying to control the uncontrollable.

I can decide how I act.

No one can control other people or events.

....

....

....

....

....

....

....

....

....

....

ANTICIPATION

Anticipation (the state of being worried *before* a specific event occurs and predicting a negative experience) is incredibly typical of worriers. This waiting process is normal and common and we all experience it, but sucks up so much time and energy! Many people remain in this agonized and uncomfortable state (which can be like purgatory) *until* the event happens. This is unfortunate. Anticipation ultimately ends up being a complete waste of time because the event almost always turns out fine! After all, the worst-case scenario is always statistically the least likely one. Often, we have amnesia and repeatedly forget that things generally have a way of working out. This is the nature of anxiety and worry—it can erase our memory of past successes (which are overwhelmingly more common than losses and disasters).

Write about a time when you spent a ton of time anticipating something. How did it actually turn out?

....

....

....

....

....

....

Looking back, how might you have spent the time more rewardingly than worrying? (Hint: Visualize the situation turning out well—then go turn on Netflix!)

....

....

....

....

....

MANAGING ANTICIPATORY ANXIETY

Don't shield yourself with worst-case scenario thinking—it does not protect you from worst-case scenarios! Instead, visualize things turning out fine. If you can change the narrative in your mind, you can save yourself from wasting precious time on unproductive worry. Remember, anticipation itself is always way worse than reality, and it would be ideal if you could opt out of the anticipation phase completely or at least shorten its duration. You can spend this time far more rewardingly. Think of the things you could get done if your brain didn't linger in Anticipation Land!

Review these statements; what are some others that could help you?

The worst-case scenario is always the least likely one.

Statistics are on my side. Anticipation is always worse than reality.

I will not waste time in Anticipation Land. I'm getting out of there!

I do not have any evidence that things are going to turn out poorly.

Why waste time worrying?

AMBIGUITY (WHEN THINGS ARE NOT CLEAR)

An ambiguous situation is one that is hard to get a read on. For example, your friend has what you interpret as an "upset" expression on their face; you send a text but do not get a quick response. Or you are waiting to hear back about something (like an acceptance letter.) In the absence of information, sometimes our imaginations run wild and we assume there are negative explanations for something that is not entirely clear. In those moments, we would like clarity immediately, but this can't always happen.

Thankfully, the absence of information is not the same as actual information, so try to avoid jumping to conclusions. It may be super tempting to try to generate an explanation (this can be a comforting strategy), but it is far better to totally accept that you just don't have an answer . . . yet. Further, the "answer" is probably something totally benign (like your friend isn't mad at you at all, just preoccupied with something else).

Write about a time when you were in an ambiguous situation that felt uncomfortable or caused you considerable distress. Describe how you felt and whether you predicted a negative outcome. Did anticipating disaster help the situation or just make it more unpleasant?

TOLERATING AMBIGUITY

Tolerating ambiguity requires patience. This is a muscle that can be built, with practice! It involves sitting with the situation and preventing yourself from jumping to wild conclusions. You can also try reminding yourself that even if something doesn't work out, it is going to be okay—you can cope. Further, it is helpful to remind yourself that ambiguity does not equal disaster. Ambiguous situations are rarely truly threatening—they are simply things that are going to be resolved or worked out over time.

Here are some statements that can help you deal with ambiguous situations. Can you add to this list?

The absence of information is not equivalent to a bad outcome.

Reality check—what does common sense tell you about this type of situation?

Just because something is unclear does not mean that it is dangerous.

Patience is the key to less worry—take a breath.

Do not make up ideas to explain why you haven't heard back. Resist the temptation!

....

....

....

....

....

....

....

....

....

....

"NECESSARY" WORRYING

We may (often subconsciously) believe that worrying actually works for us in some way. We might even think it is necessary to help us get things done or be productive. For example, you might believe that worrying intensely about an upcoming test or presentation helps you perform better and that you couldn't get a good grade otherwise. Psychologists call this *meta-worry* because it involves thinking about our thinking and worrying about our worry. Meta-worry is an aspect of metacognition, a fancy psych term that describes being aware of one's thoughts and thought processes and having beliefs about them.

Many people are superstitiously convinced that worrying about something will help improve the outcome of a situation or protect them from danger. Other kinds of meta-worries include the notion that you are unable to control your worry, that worrying will damage your body or health, that analyzing your worry will reveal some essential truth, and that any sign of anxiety that you experience indicates a real threat. These meta-worry beliefs are incredibly common, but often completely faulty.

List some ways you believe your worry helps you. Do you have any other beliefs about worrying and if so, what are they?

....

....

....

....

....

What, if anything, would happen if you stopped worrying?

....

....

....

....

....

....

REJECTING WORRY

While worry can sometimes be a little bit motivating sometimes, there are *far* more effective ways to motivate yourself (i.e. self-encouragement), and you are quite capable of being productive even if you are completely calm (more likely, in fact!).

TBH, what is worrying good for? Absolutely nothing! Thoughts do not influence what happens in the physical world. (Just try thinking "Stand up! Stand up!" over and over. When you find that your body hasn't moved, you will realize that thoughts do not lead to change unless you actively decide to change.) In the same vein, thinking something does not make it true. (Imagine you thought that purple was the best color. Does that make this a fact?)

Further, you have far more control over your worry than you think you do. This book is full of scientifically based tips and tools that demonstrate that while you cannot eliminate anxiety completely, you *can* manage and cope with it. Finally, worry is not dangerous or indicative of a real threat. It may be annoying and uncomfortable, but it does not harm the body.

Read these statements and add your own:

Worry is not uncontrollable—there are things I can do to manage it.

The presence of anxiety does not indicate that something bad is going to happen.

Worrying may be unpleasant and annoying, but it is not damaging.

Worry does not actually help me prepare for anything—it just stresses me out.

I don't need to worry in order to get my work done.

Worry does not keep me safe.

....

....

....

....

....

....

UNFOLLOW YOUR WORRY

You may be spending a lot of time fighting with your worry thoughts or trying to get them to stop. Defusing worry is a tactic in which instead of actively engaging with your worries, you detach yourself from, or unfollow them. Defusion is a strategy that asks you to look at your worry thoughts simply as mental activity in your brain. You become an observer of your thoughts rather than a victim of them. This involves mindfully noticing thoughts without judging or reacting to them. Research shows that people who stop attempting suppress worry and simply mindfully notice their worry thoughts and feelings feel more calm.

It can be incredibly helpful to use imagery and metaphors to assist you with defusion (the strategy of empowered, mindful detachment from worry and other negative emotions). The following are examples of this:

- Picture your worry as a leaf going down a stream, a ball going into a net, a package going down a conveyor belt (or anything else that moves). Let it float away.

- Imagine that you are a mountain. Your worries are clouds surrounding the mountain. Storms may come and go but the mountain is unaffected. You are strong. You notice the clouds but they do not bother you. Like a mountain, you remain rooted and steadfast.

- Think of your worry like a wave in the ocean. You can surf this wave and allow it to come down on its own. Ride the wave of your anxiety, knowing it is going to pass. You are riding this wave instead of being wiped out by it. Hang ten!

- Imagine you are the judge of a reality music show like *The Voice*. Each worry comes to the stage to "perform," and you are not satisfied. Examine each worry that comes up and quickly dismiss each one as you say: "Thank you. Next!"

- Pretend each worry is a person in a Zoom meeting and you are the moderator. Click "mute" on each worry one by one and witness the noise of each worry fade away . . . then leave the meeting altogether.

- Think of your own calming imagery, and imagine each worry as something outside of you that passes by or floats away.

DEFUSING WORRY

How do you defuse your worry thoughts? Notice that you are having them and label them "thinking." Examine them from a distance. Do not engage with them. After all, panicking or overreacting to worry thoughts can only make them stronger. For this moment, you are merely noticing the fact that you are worried without judging it or reacting to this. To defuse your worries, simply identify that a worry thought is just a thought and that is okay.

For some anxious people, defusion is a very effective approach because it removes the element of control. Instead of trying to control (modify) your thoughts and feelings, you are allowing them to be present. You accept that there is nothing wrong with having negative thoughts or feelings; letting your thoughts simply exist as they are can be incredibly freeing. Research shows that mindfully giving yourself permission to have a thought, versus trying to suppress it, can be a remarkably effective coping strategy for anxiety.

Read through the phrases below and come up with some of your own to try.

I am having the thought that _____

I am having the belief that _____

My anxiety is telling me that _____

My brain is suggesting the idea that _____

There my mind goes again!

DISCOMFORT

There is no question that anxiety is uncomfortable! Discomfort is an aspect of life that pretty much everyone dislikes and would prefer to avoid. Anxiety can be especially uncomfortable, physically and emotionally. Often when we worry about things, we are worrying about some potential scenario that *might make us uncomfortable*, and we fear that the discomfort will be incredibly unpleasant and even intolerable.

Think about the ways that the things you worry about are essentially things that might make you uncomfortable.

Some situations and/or people that make me uncomfortable:

◊

◊

◊

Some thoughts and feelings that make me uncomfortable:

◊

◊

◊

TOLERATING DISCOMFORT

In reality, while discomfort is certainly never pleasant, it is always tolerable. We experience and tolerate discomfort on a near-daily basis. We may get up earlier than we want to, wait in line for hours for concert tickets, hold an intense yoga position, and generally experience illness, fatigue, or inconvenience in some shape or form nearly every day. We grumble about it and get through it. We #persist. If you are a human being who is alive, you are not a stranger to discomfort. And when it comes to anxiety and worry, the truth is *you can handle it!*

You can cope with anxiety—the feelings and sensations that come along with it can be managed with coping strategies. Further, if the absolute worst thing that could happen in a particular situation is that *you might be uncomfortable*, remember— that is not so bad!

Read these statements, then think of some things you can tell yourself that will help you tolerate discomfort (including anxiety).

I am no stranger to discomfort; I deal with and manage discomfort on a daily basis.

The last time I felt anxious and uncomfortable, I didn't like it, but I got through it and then soon forgot all about it.

Being uncomfortable is a part of life that can't be avoided.

Coping with being uncomfortable makes me a stronger and more resilient person.

The cold never bothered me anyway . . .

....

....

....

....

....

....

....

JUDGING YOUR WORRY

Anxiety doesn't always make sense, but the fact that it isn't logical doesn't mean your experiences aren't valid. Judging or rejecting your anxious thoughts or feelings (telling yourself they aren't okay to have) can backfire by making them even more intense! (Research shows that it can lead to a rebound effect.) While it is all too common to feel upset at ourselves for being anxious ("I shouldn't be feeling this way."), scolding yourself for being worried only makes you even more worked up. Similarly, when someone else urges you to "just calm down" when you are anxious, it only makes you feel worse.

The truth is that worry may not always be justified, but it is *always* understandable. There are likely many legitimate reasons you are feeling this way. Perhaps you had a bad experience that makes this worry understandable. For example, if you got stuck in an elevator once, it makes total sense that you might be scared of elevators (even though the chances of this ever happening again are extremely low).

Further, it is also incredibly common to feel anxious for *absolutely no reason at all*. Sometimes anxiety can come on with no trigger—it just appears. It is biological; your body can have anxiety hiccups every now and then and produce anxious feelings randomly (as if it is running drills for the possibility of eventual danger, even when there is none). Therefore, judging yourself for having anxiety is misplaced. It is not your fault!

Have you ever pressured yourself to "just get over it," or told yourself that you were stupid for having anxiety (or other negative emotions)? Can you recall any moments in your life where other people told you that your anxious (or other) feelings were not valid and that you were overreacting? Did it help or did you become more upset?

Describe how you feel when this occurs:

....

....

....

....

....

....

RESISTING JUDGMENT

You are entitled to all of your feelings and emotions—they are all functional (have purpose), even if at times they are unpleasant. Your feelings are valid! Telling yourself to just stop worrying can make you more upset. Instead, allow yourself to feel your feelings. The key here is to stop trying to make your anxious thoughts and feelings go away; instead, try entering into a new (more compassionate) relationship with them. Allowing your anxious thoughts and feelings to exist can actually deflate them.

Feeling sad, stressed, worried, or frustrated is okay! We sometimes get subtle messages from other people that unpleasant emotions are to be avoided or that emotional distress is an indicator of fragile mental health. This is not true. As psychologist Lisa Damour suggests, when a situation is upsetting, your emotions put you in touch with the reality of the painful circumstance. You can then use this information, in an empowered way, to decide on a coping strategy to help yourself feel better. It is important to make room for unpleasant feelings; quite often, you can move past a difficult mood simply by giving yourself permission to have it.

Read these #copingstatements and see if you can come up with a few more that work for you.

Based on my personal experiences, my feelings make perfect sense!

My anxiety is a product of my body chemistry and life experiences—it is not my fault.

Telling myself to "just get over it" never works.

I am entitled to have the feelings that I have, even if they stress me out.

My feelings are not right or wrong—they simply are.

....

....

....

....

....

....

PHYSICAL SENSATIONS OF WORRY

Your mind and body are in frequent communication with each other, which means that anxious thoughts may be accompanied by all kinds of uncomfortable physical sensations, ranging from muscle tension to chest pains to stomach butterflies.

These sensations are a *completely normal* aspect of anxiety; all emotions have physical features. Anxiety sensations occur because our nervous system naturally produces chemicals when we are stressed. If you are prone to anxiety, you may have a slightly overactive sympathetic nervous system that produces "false alarms," or feelings of danger even when you are not actually in real peril. While these feelings can be pretty uncomfortable, they will not cause damage of any kind. Humans are resilient, and anxious sensations are highly adaptive because they are designed to alert us to and protect us from danger (even if there is none, which is often the case!).

Circle any of the physical sensations of anxiety from the list below that you have experienced, and add any others that you have felt.

Racing heart   Headache

Dizziness   Skin breakout

Nausea   Stomachache

Restlessness   Shortness of breath

Sweating   Chest tightness

Stomach butterflies   Tingly limbs

Tight jaw   Other:

Tense muscles   _____

ACCEPTING ANXIOUS SENSATIONS

It is crucial to not panic when you have anxious physical sensations. If you hyperfocus on them and feel upset about having them, the feelings may get more intense. Research shows that it is not the sensations themselves that are problematic but our *interpretations* of these sensations. If you interpret these sensations in a catastrophic way ("Oh no, I am having a heart attack!" "What the heck is happening to me?"), then you will get even more nervous and uncomfortable. Remember that feelings are JUST feelings—they are not at all dangerous. Try not to overreact to these sensations or panic when you have them. Instead, think of them calmly as interesting and informative (they are letting you know that you are having a tough moment). Be kind to yourself. Do a physical relaxation exercise (many can be found online), use a mindfulness app, or take a breathing break (page 15). Or simply do nothing and move on with your life! (Panic is a prime moment for mind over matter; actively ignoring it and moving on with your daily activities can often do the trick).

Repeat these statements to yourself, and see if you can come up with other effective examples.

These feelings are designed to keep me safe; they will not harm me.

When I feel panicked, my body is most definitely sounding a false alarm.

Emotions may be uncomfortable at times but are never dangerous.

I am not going to overreact to these sensations.

I breathe in, I breathe out.

....

....

....

....

....

RUMINATION

Rumination, or obsessing over something that bothers you, is a very common worry process. It occurs when you become preoccupied with something and are unable to get it out of your mind. You may find yourself repeatedly replaying events from the past or dwelling on something you said or did; or you might continuously fret over an upcoming event. Rumination is repetitive; your worry is running on a treadmill and it can't stop, won't stop! Rumination is also normal. To some extent, everyone ruminates on their problems and rehashes various scenarios. However, over-dwelling on a problem can cause you to get stuck in a loop and feel distressed and helpless. Overthinking hurts your happiness! Further, rumination tends to involve fixation solely on the negative, which prevents you from seeing the big picture.

Some examples of rumination:

Why do these things always happen to me?

Why am I in this situation?

Why did I do that? That was so dumb!

What if _____ happens?

This is awful. I don't know what to do about it!

Can you think of some rumination examples of your own? Or topics that you are currently obsessing about?

....

....

....

....

....

....

....

....

PROBLEM—SOLVING

Instead of ruminating on the problem, it is far more productive to think about potential solutions that could help you actually deal with the situation you are concerned about. Problem-solving is a far more helpful thinking style. It is a proactive and analytical approach to stress that promotes change—it takes you out of your worry state and gets you where you need to go! Ask yourself, "How can I solve this problem?" or "What would be a good way to manage this situation?" For past problems, try telling yourself, "That is over and I can't change it—but I could handle that type of situation differently in the future." The key here is to avoid obsessing and overthinking and instead focus on solutions. Most of the time, generating potential ways to actually deal with things that are stressing you out (for example, by making a plan or enlisting others for help) can stop rumination in its tracks.

Read these problem-solving statements, then write some that you think could work for you:

What can I do to make this better?

How can I cope with this situation?

Whom can I ask for help?

Is there a way to turn this around? What if I try _____ ?

Next time this happens, I can _____ .

....

....

....

....

....

Next, think about stressors in your life. Pick one or two. A helpful thought exercise is to envision some specific ways you can deal with, problem-solve, or manage that situation. For example, let's say a test or work presentation goes poorly. Could you speak to your teacher or boss, ask for a retake or do-over, or discuss redemptive measures such as approaching it differently next time and/or enlisting help?

INDECISION

"I so overcomplicate, people tell me to medicate," sings Ariana Grande. A common feature of worry is the feeling of being unable to make up your mind! You may go back and forth between two or more options, feeling terrified of making the wrong choice and having to deal with unpleasant or perceived severe consequences as a result. You question your own judgment. Sometimes it's related to a small thing, like picking an outfit for an event where you want to look your best; other times, it's about a bigger life decision, such as which college to attend or whether to accept a new job. No matter the situation, the feeling of not being able to make a choice (and fear of making the "wrong" one) is deeply uncomfortable and can exacerbate the experience of worry.

Write about a decision you are struggling to make:

....

....

....

....

....

....

....

....

....

....

....

....

....

....

MAKING A CHOICE

The reality is that you are perfectly capable of making reasonable to excellent decisions! You have done this your entire life and it has almost always turned out fine. For those times when it didn't, remember that not everyone can get it right all the time, and that's okay. Everyone has to roll the dice, take a chance, and see what happens. Technically, there is no "wrong" decision—only valuable learning experiences. If (when) you make a choice that doesn't end well, you will handle it, learn from it, and it won't be the end of the world. Very few things are irreversible or completely catastrophic. Damage control can always be done! What's the big deal?

Delaying decisions can drive up your anxiety by worsening rumination. The more you put off making a decision about something, the more you convince yourself that a bad choice would be ruinous. The most effective way to resolve indecision is quite simply to make a decision—quickly. Consulting someone else can be helpful, as long as you do not rely on this excessively (lest you convince yourself you are not capable of making decisions on your own). Take a deep breath. Make a choice, own it, and test it out to see what happens! Or as Thanos said in *Avengers: Infinity War*: "The hardest choices require the strongest wills."

Read these statements. Can you add some others to aid you in future decision-making?

It is okay to have trouble making up my mind, but having a decision made will make me feel so much better!

I have solid judgment and I can make good decisions.

Nothing truly bad will happen if my decision is not perfect.

If I am not sure about something, I can ask for advice.

I can just pick something and put this behind me!

....

....

....

....

....

FEELING OVERWHELMED

Often we have too much going on at once. It might be a big, complicated project or maybe you have numerous obligations, such as promises to family and friends or assignments all due at once. You might become worried that you cannot handle all (or any) of it. Perhaps you are trying to avoid thinking about it at all or panic when you do think about it. Quite possibly, you cannot figure out how to approach it or even where to begin. Or you might think about it obsessively but not be able to take action. When there is a lot going on, your surge capacity or emotional band-width may be reduced, which can make it a little harder to cope.

In these instances, your best bet for stress management is to slow down and take a breath. Chances are, there is a way to break this situation down into more manageable parts. Perhaps you could even delegate some of the tasks or ask other people for help. Feeling overwhelmed can also be a sign that you are burned out and may need to incorporate a self-care practice into your life (such as yoga, exercise, hobbies, time with a pet) or give yourself specific breaks and downtime to decompress.

Here is a thought exercise: think about something (or things) overwhelming you right now. How have you been coping? Is there a calmer, more organized way to approach these things? Brainstorm how you could break it down into smaller steps or components and/or identify people in your life who could help you (i.e. help you study, run an errand for you, do a chore for you as a favor). Can you give yourself permission to take a short, calming break? If so, what could you do?

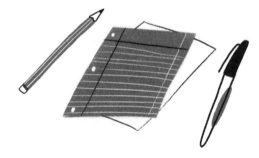

PLANNING AHEAD

If something feels too big or overwhelming, a great trick is to break it down into smaller, more manageable pieces—essentially, by making a plan. Planning ahead is also effective when you have too much to do and too little time. In this instance, it can be helpful to make a schedule or an outline for completing various tasks.

For example, if you have a report due with lots of research and citations, do not panic. Make a schedule for yourself; count the number of days until the deadline and select one or two tasks to do each day. For instance:

Days 1–2: Read and take notes. Days 3–4: Sort notes.
Day 5: Make an outline. Days 6–8: Write three pages each day.

This is called chunking, since you are breaking something bigger into more digestible chunks, which is a hugely helpful part of planning and managing your life.

Some situations that make you feel freaked out may be more emotionally overwhelming, such as an upcoming surgery or a complicated social situation. Try to vividly imagine yourself in the situation (don't avoid thinking about it!). Make a plan for what you will do before, during, and afterward. Psychologists call this "coping ahead." Think of enlisting others for support. Tell yourself it is going to be okay!

A caveat: Plan, but do not overplan. Do not excessively overthink about the situation. Make the plan and then move on, knowing you have a strategy in place.

Here are some statements to help you "cope ahead." See if you can think of more.

It is normal to feel overwhelmed—life can be overwhelming!

One thing at a time.

Everything big can be broken into smaller components.

I can tackle this piece by piece.

I can ask for help. People would love to help me out!

ADVERSITY (WHEN LIFE GIVES YOU LEMONS)

Life is unfair. Some problems cannot be solved, and disastrous events occur that are beyond our control. If you are alive and human, you are inevitably going to encounter adversity—times that just completely suck. Breakups, illnesses, moves, and other kinds of loss are inevitable parts of living.

When things are intensely stressful, feeling worried and distressed is completely normal and understandable. A typical response is to wonder, "Why is this happening to me?" or to feel that the circumstances in which you find yourself are completely intolerable and must be escaped. While this is a natural reaction, saying these things to yourself, unfortunately, is likely to make you feel even more agitated. This kind of hopeless self-talk, while totally understandable, will only serve to exacerbate your distress about a situation that can't be modified, at a time when the last thing you need is to be more upset!

In fact, rejecting the reality of what you are facing does not cause the reality to change. Feeling angry and bitter (even if understandable) takes a LOT of emotional energy. It is exhausting to spend time bemoaning something that you can't change. The world is unjust, but fixating on the unfairness just makes us even more miserable. In these kinds of circumstances, the best way to tackle anxiety is through empowered acceptance.

Think about something in your life that has made or is making you truly miserable. What aspect of the situation cannot be changed (right now)? Imagine what it would feel like to stop fighting with this fact.

PRACTICING ACCEPTANCE

Acceptance is making an empowered choice to peacefully accept rather than to fight against a painful situation. It is best for circumstances where truly not much, or nothing, can be done about a predicament that we hate. Acceptance means that even though we may actively despise what's happening, we can acknowledge that it is in fact happening and it is not great. Acceptance does not mean approval! It is simply a way to reduce the suffering and immense frustration that comes from trying to change a situation that cannot be changed.

The key thing to remember is that the pain of life is unavoidable, but suffering (dwelling, rejecting reality, bitterly complaining) is *optional*.

How does one practice acceptance? It involves a powerful perspective shift. Acceptance is understanding that something sucks *and* there isn't much you can do about it AND that is okay. Once you have reduced the "noise" that comes from the agony of focusing on how much you hate a given circumstance, you can better use your energy on getting through it, especially if the situation brings you anxiety.

Read through these statements to practice acceptance, and think of some that are specific to you or that you might tell a loved one who is going through a tough time.

This situation massively sucks, but focusing on how much I hate it makes me feel worse.

Rejecting reality does not change reality.

Acceptance does not mean approval.

Accepting something will free my mental space for effective coping.

Pain is unavoidable, but suffering is optional.

....

....

....

....

....

....

BIGGER PICTURE

Another helpful strategy for managing stress and adverse circumstances is to look at the bigger picture. Often, when we worry, we disqualify the positive—we can't see all the things that are going well, or even simply okay. We zoom in on the negative and conclude that everything is terrible and awful. This does not indicate that stress isn't legitimate; simply, it can be helpful to remind ourselves that there are other things going on in our lives to balance it out.

Psychologists have found that focusing on aspects of our lives that are incredibly important to us (and that make us truly happy) can be extremely helpful for managing anxiety and other negative emotions. Research has found that identifying your values (things that have meaning to you) is far more satisfying than focusing exclusively on your goals (things you want to accomplish). For example, a goal might be "lose weight," while a value might be "be healthy." The value is much more meaningful (and attainable) than the goal. Values are things that really mean a lot to you in your life, that fit in with your vision of who you are and what you are most proud of. A few examples of values include having health, being a good friend or a good family member, being honest, being kind, promoting equality, having spirituality, among others. Before concluding that this is extremely cheesy, consider what channeling these valuable and meaningful things might do for your mood and specifically, your anxiety level!

Look in your heart—who/what is most important to you? What do you truly care the most about? At the end of your days, how will you want to have lived the moments of your life? Does listening to all of your worry thoughts take you where you want to go? Identify and list some of your values. Do you think focusing on these will help you feel less stressed and more fulfilled?

....

....

....

....

....

....

FLIP THE SWITCH ON YOUR WORRY

When we feel anxious or worried, it can be preoccupying. Our attention is fixated on all the things that are going wrong in our lives, and we get trapped in a negative headspace. It is not surprising, then, that anxiety and depression can go hand in hand. This occurs when we feel helpless (and hopeless). In these moments, a conscious attentional shift may be warranted. The strategy here is to get your mind off your worry by gently shifting your attention away from what is bothering you and instead attending more consciously to things going on that are positive or neutral. This can be useful, in particular, when worry is keeping you up at night or preventing you from falling asleep (2:00 a.m. is not the ideal time to dwell on our stress).

It can be helpful to remind yourself of the things in your life that are actually going neutrally or well (versus worrisome or terrible)—because sometimes we forget all about them! You need to change the channel. Imagine you have been watching a YouTube channel titled "Everything Is Awful." What if instead you closed that window and tuned in to a channel titled "Everything Is Awesome?" (pretend you're in that LEGO movie). You would feel so much better. You do not necessarily need to tell yourself that everything is truly awesome (being overly positive can backfire), but you *can* at least remember that things are pretty good, and certainly could be so much worse.

Review the following coping statements and see if you can generate more of your own:

There are many things in my life that are going well.

Focusing solely on the negative is not good for my mood.

Look at the bigger picture.

This too shall pass. . . . Now would be nice!

Let me remind myself of at least one thing that I enjoy doing.

....

....

....

....

....

AVOIDANCE

When you feel worried about things, a natural instinct is to try to avoid them! Most of us routinely spend time and energy trying to avoid anxiety-provoking *situations* as well as uncomfortable and distressing *thoughts and feelings.*

However, the truth is that anxiety and avoidance are best friends—they are in a close partnership. This is because avoidance eliminates your opportunity to learn that *if you actually face the situation you are worried about, it would be fine!* Escaping the situation (even temporarily) actually makes anxiety worse, not better.

Avoidance works its evil magic by reinforcing your belief that you just cannot handle a stressful situation and denying you the chance to master it and learn that it is not as scary as you think. For example, imagine you need to ask for an extension on a project but you are worried that the conversation is going to be stressful—so you put it off. When you procrastinate, you experience instant relief that you aren't doing the difficult thing. Whew!! This can be addictive and reinforcing. However, after that momentary relief, your worry goes right back up. Further, the worry will be even more intense now because your last memory was how amazing it felt to avoid the difficult thing, which makes approaching it *seem* more insurmountable in your mind.

Think about situations or worries that you have been avoiding dealing with because they make you anxious. Do you think that avoidance is helping you or hurting you?

Write about a time in your life when you faced something you were worried about and it turned out okay.

FACING FEAR

If you brave your feelings of anxiety and face a difficult situation head-on, the outcome will be entirely different. You will still experience some short-lived anxiety at first, but once you actually approach and complete the difficult or scary thing, that anxious feeling will abate immediately. You will feel relieved and have an incredible sense of mastery. You will learn that whatever it was you were intimidated by is not that bad at all and you can handle it. The key is to tolerate the spike in worry, knowing it will be vanquished—do not let the temporary discomfort deter you!

Once you start the task you are worried about (oral presentation, difficult conversation with someone, first day of a new program), you will find that the anxiety will start to dip. Once you finish, the anxiety will be gone. This experience is far more satisfying than avoiding it! Further, it will get easier and easier with repetition and practice. A reminder here that crippling anticipation is a waste of time because things almost always turn out just fine.

Read through these statements to cope with avoidance. Can you add some of your own?

Avoidance is really just a fake solution to my worry.

If I face this situation, it will not be nearly as bad as I think it is going to be.

Dealing with the thing I'm avoiding is the most effective way to achieve relief.

My anxiety will not remain high forever; it will always come down.

Practice really does make perfect—the more that I do something hard, the easier it will become.

....

....

....

....

....

....

PERFECTIONISM

No discussion of worry can be complete without examining perfectionism. Many of us who tend to worry are closeted perfectionists. Perfectionism isn't always obvious; it can also be subtle. It is not always about getting perfect scores or having perfect handwriting. It can also be found in your expectations. Do you expect things to work out perfectly all the time? Do you fear making mistakes and hate any form of failure? Are you always seeking approval and aim for every person to like you, all of the time? This can be a heavy burden!

The fundamental problem here is that perfection is impossible. It only exists in the dictionary. No one can perform perfectly on every test, have a perfect body, a perfect family, a perfect social life, or a perfect job. Wanting these things is engaging in wishful thinking! Further, it is unfortunate that there is often subtle pressure out there to be perfect. Perfectionism creates intense stress because it involves chasing the unattainable—absolutely no one is perfect. Embracing *imperfection* is the key to a more relaxing and peaceful existence. Life is full of glitches!

Note on social perfectionism: Remember, it is not possible to be liked by everyone at all times. Haters are just more people paying attention to you! Being occasionally disliked is not a big deal and will in no way affect where you are going in life. You can handle it!

Think of an example of a recent "imperfection" in your life. What would it be like to just be okay with it? Make a list of all the things in your life that you expect to be or would like to be perfect (and reflect on how realistic each one is).

GOOD ENOUGH

Imperfection is the norm in life, so we may as well get used to it. Tolerating imperfection does not mean giving up or having low standards—it means merely modifying them. The goal here is to replace perfect with "good enough."

Perfectionism often involves avoidance. If you think anything you do has to be absolutely perfect, this vastly increases the pressure on you and the anxiety you have about the task at hand, and may make you more likely to put off doing things. (This is why procrastination is really an anxiety issue and not a laziness issue!) Beware of the Perfection Monster that can wreak havoc on your life.

Perfectionists evaluate themselves and others critically, judging their work or behavior emotionally and assigning value (frequently negative) to the performance of themselves and others. What if you instead try to assess things neutrally, describing the person, situation, or thing using entirely factual terms and attempting to remain as neutral as possible? When we use facts (versus emotions) to describe a situation, this description ends up being far more accurate—especially if we apply these more fair and balanced standards to ourselves. For example, if you think a performance went abysmally, instead focus on what actually happened ("I did the 'Renegade' challenge on TikTok and I got almost every move correct—it is difficult to do this dance perfectly!")

Think about the statements below and try to continue the list with "good enough" coping statements that you can use.

Perfection is impossible—it only exists in the dictionary.

If perfection is always my goal, I will always be frustrated and miserable.

Doing something imperfectly will not kill me or ruin my life.

Embracing imperfection is healthy!

If I use only critical terms to describe my performance, my assessment will be biased and not accurate.

....

....

....

....

COMPARISON

Have you ever heard the expression, "Comparison is the thief of joy?" It is true!

Comparing ourselves to other people (in terms of looks, smarts, talent, popularity, wealth, or activities) has skyrocketed with the rise of social media. It is easy to conclude that your peers and acquaintances (and their friends and relatives) are doing waaaay better than you when they post their highlights and seem to be living their best lives every single day. It is impossible not to experience FOMO occasionally and feel demoralized, even if you are a highly confident person. This experience can create intense worry and preoccupation, as well as bring on feelings of sadness, insecurity, and distress.

When we compare ourselves to other people, we typically make "downward" comparisons, in which we conclude that we are not as good as others. Downward comparisons tend to be inaccurate because we are typically way too hard on ourselves. While it may feel weird to remind yourself that you are doing better than (at least some) other people, this may be necessary to find balance and to remind yourself that you are doing okay. It is best to resist comparisons completely, but if you are going to engage in them, try to be fair in your comparisons.

Imagine what it would be like to stop engaging in social comparison. With whom would you stop comparing yourself to? Do you think you would be happier? In what ways are you doing okay (or even great)? Write about a person or people to whom you have compared yourself lately. How does this make you feel about yourself and your life? Do you know for sure that this person is doing better?

FOCUSING ON YOURSELF

When you are comparing yourself to someone else you idealize, it is practically guaranteed that you do not have all the facts. You are not seeing this person on a bad day, in the midst of a stressful time, or during an ordinary moment where basically nothing is happening. Such moments make up the majority of life and they are definitely not being presented.

When people post on social media, you have no way of knowing the context of the situation. Perhaps two people are grinning in a photo but moments earlier ended a vicious argument. Maybe someone seems to be on a glamorous trip, but the photo does not capture the bug bites, the fighting, the flat tire, the cold weather, or the plane that was delayed by six hours.

Try to resist comparing yourself to others—it ruins your happiness! Stop the comparisons completely and focus on yourself. You are doing great.

Take a mini social media break. Try to limit excessive scrolling. Perhaps give yourself a reasonable time limit. You can tell you have hit a point of burnout or oversaturation with the scrolling when you start to feel upset or badly about yourself. At this moment, it is time to walk away and do something else, even for a few minutes. Take a breath. Remember that no one's life is perfect.

Consider these statements when you are tempted to compare; add some that are meaningful to you.

Don't make assumptions about other people based solely on the information presented.

I can never know for sure what someone else's situation is.

People always put their best foot forward and conceal less-appealing moments of their lives.

Downward comparisons are never accurate.

The best way to have confidence is to refrain from engaging in comparisons and to focus on myself. I am doing great.

....

....

....

FAILURE

Worry tends to be dramatic. A classic example is when you worry that you are going to completely fail at something or when you tell yourself, "I am a failure." This is almost certainly untrue. Failure, like perfection, is mostly a construct (it's not real). With some exceptions (yes, it is possible to fail a test), there is really no such thing as failure. When we use the word "failure" (such a harsh word!), it rarely actually applies to the situation at hand, even if it genuinely feels that way. Imagine someone you care about moans to you, "I am such a failure!!!" Is that person really one? Are you?

Failing at something is always a very low-probability event, which is ironic since we often worry about this a LOT. Further, there is an unfortunate attitude in our society that failure is to be avoided at all costs and that one should try hard to never make mistakes (even if we are also told it is okay to make mistakes). These conflicting messages are confusing!

In fact, mistakes are completely unavoidable, inevitable, and honorable. If you are alive, you are going to make mistakes consistently and frequently, and fall flat on your face periodically. When this occurs, people tend to feel devastated and very upset with themselves—but this recrimination is unnecessary. You are absolutely allowed to make mistakes!! Further, you are *supposed* to make them. The nerve cells in the brain develop stronger connections with every learning experience, and errors are the best teachers. Mistakes are remarkably effective and powerful motivators that help us consistently improve our strategies and our behavior over time. (This is why older people are pretty wise.)

Failure and mistakes can be wonderful teachers. Try this thought exercise: Reflect about a handful of times you have thought you failed (or actually did fail something)—or think about the latest mistake you made. What did this experience help you figure out? How did you recover from the mistake?

MISTAKES ARE OKAY!

Mistakes are incredible sources of information. They tell us what not to do next time and what to avoid in the future. How are you supposed to know this otherwise!? (We have established in this book that you are not a mind reader!) Albert Einstein famously said, "A person who never made a mistake never tried anything new." In the moment, making a mistake may feel awful, but eventually, you will look back on the situation and be cool with what you found out and where it led you.

A word about regret. Regret is the emotion we experience when we berate ourselves for doing something that we feel did not turn out well and wish deeply that we had not done it. Regret is a waste of time because the event has already happened. It is in the past, and all you can do is try to do better next time. Let it go and move on!

Similarly, be sure to avoid unnecessary guilt or shame and remind yourself that messing up does not make you a bad person! Allowing yourself the learning experience of mistakes is a major step toward a less anxious life.

Read these statements when you are worried about mistakes or failing. Can you add to this list?

When I believe I am a failure, I need to examine the evidence.

Most setbacks are not the end of the world.

The present crisis is always the worst crisis. It, too, will pass.

Failure is a wonderful teacher. I can learn incredible things from my mistakes.

Screwing up is a part of life that can't be avoided—and it is actually pretty badass.

....

....

....

....

....

....

SELF—CRITICISM

Many of us have been raised to believe that being hard on oneself is the most effective way to motivate ourselves. We all have an inner critic who lives inside our brain and never lets us feel like we're good enough. However, that inner critic is wrong! Research shows that self-compassion (being kind to yourself) is far more effective than self-criticism in motivating changes in our behavior. Criticizing yourself basically only makes you feel terrible—and doesn't change the outcome. According to research by psychologist Kristin Neff, criticism of yourself under-mines your confidence and causes the body to release the stress hormone cortisol—and no one thrives under stress.

Imagine your inner critic is a real hater who likes to throw shade at you—it gives you way more dislikes than likes. Your inner critic frequently assigns you only one or two stars—even though anyone with the internet can write a bad review!

In contrast, self-compassion provides optimal conditions for learning from mistakes and making better choices. Self-compassion is not indulgent; it is stra-tegic thinking and good science! Research shows that self-compassionate people are more self-confident, more resilient, more likely to persist and try again when failure occurs, and overall are better able to cope with life.

List a few things that you consistently criticize yourself for. Think about these criticisms rationally. Are you really that bad? Is it possible that your inner critic is totally wrong about you? What if, instead, you believed and trusted your inner coach to cheer you on?

Consider something going on in your life that you are being really hard on your-self for or feeling incredibly disappointed about. What could you say to yourself about it that would be really kind? What might you tell a friend or loved one in the same situation? Can you extend that same compassion toward yourself?

BE KIND TO YOURSELF

Self-compassion involves identifying when you are having a moment of suffering, and comforting yourself. An essential part of this practice is reminding yourself that *everyone* suffers and you are not the only one.

Self-compassion feels amazing. It provides a grounding experience and calms you down enough to enable you to think clearly about a problem. It is also an incredibly reliable strategy, since we cannot always count on other people to validate our feelings or say the exact right thing to us—while we DO know what to say to ourselves that will help us feel better. You always have a choice—you can feel guilty and terrible about doing something wrong, OR you can flood yourself with compassion and tell yourself that it is understandable that this happened and you will do better next time.

Some effective methods of practicing self-compassion include positive self-talk (#copingstatements!), soothing movement and touch (try gently rubbing your arms or holding your hand over your heart). The use of supportive and comforting self-talk is especially key for letting go of self-judgment, silencing your inner critic, cultivating self-compassion, and reducing anxiety.

Read through these self-compassionate coping statements. How many more can you come up with?

Self-compassion is more effective than self-criticism in motivating behavior change.

Being unkind to myself does not accomplish anything.

If I practice self-compassion, my mood will be so much better.

If I can be compassionate toward others, I can be compassionate toward myself.

Life is difficult for everyone (not just me.)

....

....

....

....

....

DELVE DEEPER

SELECTED RESOURCES
AND FURTHER READING

THE SKILLS IN THIS BOOK are informed by the following therapy approaches:

COGNITIVE BEHAVIORAL THERAPY (CBT)

ACCEPTANCE AND COMMITMENT THERAPY (ACT)

DIALECTICAL BEHAVIOR THERAPY (DBT)

MINDFULNESS-BASED STRESS REDUCTION (MBSR)

COMPASSION-FOCUSED THERAPY (CFT)

These types of therapy are all supported by research as being very effective in providing relief for a variety of emotional difficulties, including anxiety.

Goodbye, Anxiety is a compilation of over twenty years of my experience as a therapist and can be considered the "greatest hits" of what I believe works best for helping young people with anxiety. While some therapists prefer to stick to one approach (each of these treatments has been studied in isolation in psychology research labs to make sure it is effective), in clinical practice, many therapists utilize elements of ALL of these approaches to different degrees and tailor the therapy to what the client needs. As a therapist who also struggles with anxiety (who doesn't?), I myself use these skills, and I try to teach all of them to help the people I work with—because the tools utilized in these approaches are terrific, and at least one of them is going to help you feel better!

In this section you will find some resources that you may find useful for anxiety and mood management, including websites for locating a therapist. The remaining resources, along with this book, can be considered "self-help." Feel free to review this list and check out what appeals to you! For additional helpful resources for anxiety management, including apps, videos, podcasts, and social media accounts, please visit my website, DrTerriBacow.com.

HOW TO FIND A THERAPIST

ABCT (Association for Behavioral and Cognitive Therapies): Has a "Find a CBT Therapist (FAT)" search engine. FindCBT.org/FAT.

ADAA (Anxiety and Depression Association of America): Has a "Find a Therapist" directory (therapists who are members of ADAA). Members.adaa.org/page/FATMain.

Advekit: Get matched to a therapist. Available in eight states. Works with some insurances. Advekit.com.

APA Locator (American Psychological Association): Type in a zip code or a city and state to find a psychologist near you. To further refine your search, type in the name of a provider or the specialty for which you'd like help. Locator.APA.org.

IOCDF (International OCD Foundation): Has a "Find Help" webpage where you can search for therapists and other resources related to OCD. IOCDF.org/find-help.

Psychology Today: Has a general search engine for finding therapists. PsychologyToday.com.

Zencare: A great new search engine for finding therapists, especially those who offer telehealth. Currently only offered in the United States. The therapists are vetted by the founders. Zencare.co.

FURTHER READING

BOOKS FOR ADOLESCENTS

Bradshaw, Cheryl M. *The Resilience Workbook for Teens: Activities to Help You Gain Confidence, Manage Stress, and Cultivate a Growth Mindset.* Oakland, CA: New Harbinger Publications, 2019.

Eich, Jean. *Dialectical Behavior Therapy Skills Training with Adolescents: A Practical Workbook for Therapists, Teens & Parents.* Eau Claire, WI: PESI Publishing, 2015.

March, John. *Talking Back to OCD: The Program That Helps Kids and Teens Say "No Way"—and Parents Say "Way to Go."* New York: Guilford Press, 2007.

May, Jill Ehrenreich, Sarah M. Kennedy, Jamie A. Sherman, Shannon M. Bennett, and David H. Barlow. *Unified Protocol for Transdiagnostic Treatment of Emotional Disorders in Adolescents: Workbook (Treatments That Work).* New York: Oxford University Press, 2010.

Micco, Jamie A. *The Worry Workbook for Teens: Effective CBT Strategies to Break the Cycle of Chronic Worry and Anxiety.* Oakland, CA: New Harbinger Publications, 2017.

Pincus, Donna B., Jill T. Ehrenreich, and David A. Spiegel. *Riding the Wave Workbook.* New York: Oxford University Press, 2008.

Schab, Lisa M. *The Self-Esteem Workbook for Teens: Activities to Help You Build Confidence and Achieve Your Goals.* Oakland, CA: New Harbinger Publications, 2013.

Shannon, Jennifer. *The Shyness and Social Anxiety Workbook for Teens: CBT and ACT Skills to Help You Build Social Confidence.* Oakland, CA: New Harbinger Publications, 2012.

Turrell, Sheri L. *The Mindfulness and Acceptance Workbook for Teen Anxiety: Activities to Help You Overcome Fears and Worries Using Acceptance and Commitment Therapy (Instant Help Book for Teens).* Oakland, CA: New Harbinger Publications, 2018.

BOOKS FOR YOUNG ADULTS

Bourne, Edmund J. *The Anxiety and Phobia Workbook, 8th ed.* Oakland, CA: New Harbinger Publications, 2010.

Hayes, Steven C. *Get Out of Your Mind and Into Your Life: The New Acceptance and Commitment Therapy.* Oakland, CA: New Harbinger Publications, 2005.

Leahy, Robert L. *The Worry Cure: Seven Steps to Stop Worry from Worrying You.* New York: Three Rivers Press, 2005.

McKay, Matthew, Patrick Fanning, Carole Honeyburch, and Catharine Sutker. *The Self-Esteem Companion: Simple Exercises to Help You Challenge Your Inner Critic and Celebrate Your Personal Strengths.* Oakland, CA: New Harbinger Publications, 2005.

Neff, Kristin, and Christopher Germer. *The Mindful Self-Compassion Workbook: A Proven Way to Accept Yourself, Build Inner Strength, and Thrive.* Oakland, CA: New Harbinger Publications, 2018.

Spradlin, Scott E. *Don't Let Your Emotions Run Your Life: How Dialectical Behavior Therapy Can Put You in Control.* Oakland, CA: New Harbinger Publications, 2003.

LEARN MORE ABOUT ANXIETY

Anxiety Canada: AnxietyCanada.com/learn-about-anxiety/anxiety-in-youth.

National Institute of Mental Health: www.nimh.nih.gov/health/topics/anxiety-disorders/index.shtml#part_145338.